How to Draw
Cool Stuff

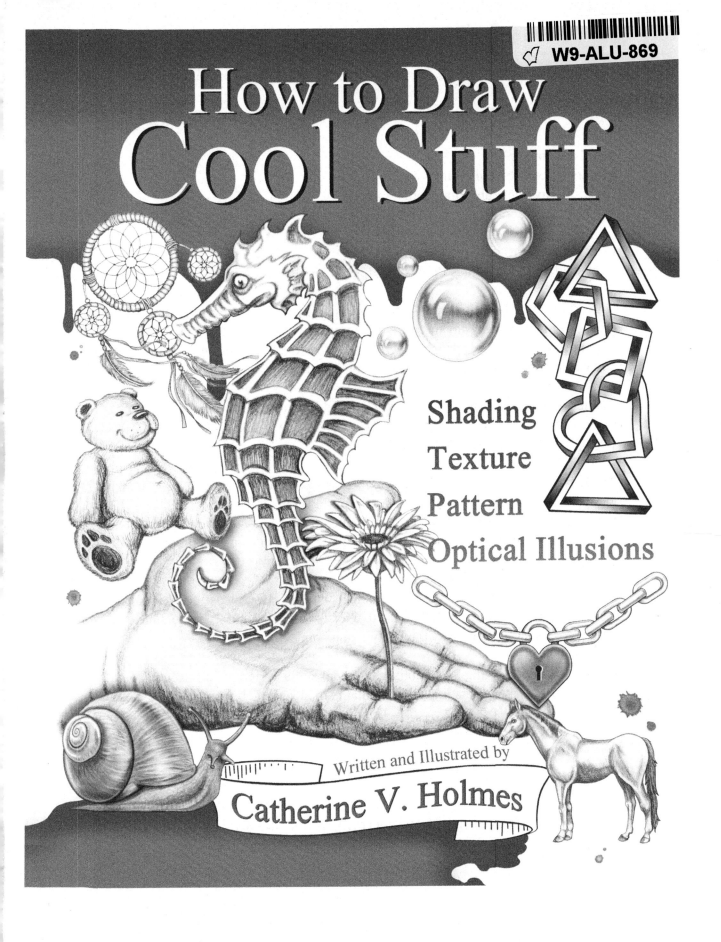

Shading

Texture

Pattern

Optical Illusions

Written and Illustrated by

Catherine V. Holmes

Published by:
Library Tales Publishing, Inc.
www.LibraryTalesPublishing.com
www.Facebook.com/LibraryTalesPublishing

For general information on our other products and services, please contact our Customer Care Department at 1-800-754-5016, or fax 917-463-0892. For technical support, please visit www.LibraryTalesPublishing.com

Library Tales Publishing also publishes its books in a variety of electronic formats. Every content that appears in print is available in electronic books.

ISBN-13: 978-0692382516
ISBN-10: 0692382518

PRINTED IN THE UNITED STATES OF AMERICA

Dedication

For my mom, Virginia Thayer, who supported me through all of the ups and downs, my dad, Kenneth Holmes, who helped me to draw great masterpieces on giant refrigerator boxes, Lisa and Tabitha for being my creative cohorts, my babies for showing me what life really means and to Jay for being there. Also, to my constant companion, Dexter.

I would like to acknowledge all the art teachers I had growing up. Without them, my soul would not be as rich. To all of the teachers I currently work with, keep doing what you are doing. You are changing the world.

HOW TO DRAW COOL STUFF
BOOK #1

PRICE: $19.99
PAPERBACK, 254 PAGES
ISBN: 978-0615991429
WWW.HOWTODRAWCOOLSTUFF.COM
WWW.FACEBOOK.COM/DRAWCOOLSTUFF

How to Draw Cool Stuff shows simple step-by-step illustrations that make it easy for anyone to draw cool stuff with precision and confidence. These pages will guide you through the basic principles of illustration by concentrating on easy-to-learn shapes that build into complex drawings. With the step-by-step guidelines provided, anything can become easy to draw. This book contains a series of fun, hands-on exercises that will help you see line, shape, space and other elements in everyday objects and turn them into detailed works of art in just a few simple steps. The exercises in this book will help train your brain so you can visualize ordinary objects in a different manner, allowing you to see through the eyes of an artist. From photorealistic faces to holiday themes and tattoo drawings, *How to Draw Cool Stuff* makes drawing easier than you would think and more fun than you ever imagined! Now is the time to learn how to draw the subjects and scenes you've always dreamt of drawing. *How to Draw Cool Stuff* is suitable for artists of any age, benefiting everyone from teachers and students to self-learners and hobbyists. *How to Draw Cool Stuff* will help you realize your artistic potential and expose you to the pure joy of drawing!

PREVIOUS TITLES

TABLE OF CONTENTS

Chapter 1
The Basics

Chapter 2
Shading

Chapter 3
Texture and Pattern

Chapter 4
Optical Illusions

Chapter 5
Cool Stuff

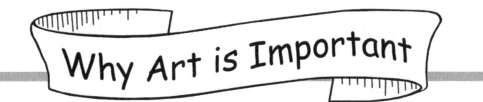

Why Art is Important

Visual art is a conversation and drawing can be your voice. What subject will you draw? What colors and medium will you choose? What are you inspired by? What story will your art-work tell? You choose what you want to say.

Learning to create things and appreciate visual aesthetics are essential to the development of well-rounded human beings. An arts-rich experience provides many advantages. Along with honed imagination and creative skills, active participants in the arts are able to express themselves and are open to new pathways for learning. Art can help us to find confidence and self-discipline, see the value of different cultures, think critically, solve problems and make informed judgments.

Through drawing, many of these attributes are exercised. From the simple act of holding a pencil which helps to develop fine motor skills in young children to an appreciation of ideas that are different from the norm, art provides a vast array of opportunities to see and interpret the world. Looking at and talking about art gets us to analyze which is a hugely important skill as we can experience our thoughts more fully and develop ideas more completely. The experience of making choices while creating art can carry over into other aspects of life, teaching us that problems can have more than one solution and that questions can have more than one answer. - CVH

About The Author

Catherine V. Holmes is a mother, animal lover, teacher, artist, youth advocate and author/illustrator of the "How to Draw Cool Stuff" series.

"We encounter art every day in every aspect of our lives. From creative problem solving to drawing interesting things to the simple appreciation of beauty, creating art is a great way of improving concentration, expressing individuality and providing pleasure for yourself. Once an artist becomes engaged in the process of making something; beautiful and unique things can happen. Often times, this process is even more valuable than the outcome. The individual growth that happens as a result of making art never stops as long as there is a desire to create. The act of drawing is a way to pass the time, relax and offers an escape from reality. Always find the time to explore new ideas and enjoy the journey of creating."

FOREWORD

Welcome to "How to Draw Cool Stuff: Basics, Shading, Texture and Pattern, Optical Illusions"; a guide for the enthusiastic artist. By having this book in your possession you are one step closer to exploring your inner creativity, honing your skills as an artist, creative problem solving, appreciating the beauty of the world around you, creating a likeness, expressing feelings visually and drawing interesting things.

The subjects included are a sampling of the basics, shading, texture, pattern, optical illusions and, of course, cool stuff. Easy to follow projects include drawing simple shapes and forms to creating complex objects and designs.

To begin, try the basic exercises in chapter one. Shape and form, which are used in the compositions of paintings and sculptures, are explored. Creating objects using basic forms simplifies the process of drawing and makes it easier to see what shapes make up a particular object. By drawing forms as part of an object, the artist is able to show depth as well as height and width.

One of the most realistic effects an artist can produce in order to make an interesting artwork is shading, discussed in chapter two. Shading is one of the easiest ways to add depth, contrast, character and movement to a drawing. There are several types of shading and many ways to go about doing it. This chapter will explain a few of these popular techniques.

Chapter three explores a variety of texture and pattern ideas that can be included in an artwork. These are two of the elements and principals of art that help to add intrigue and depth to a design. These elements are necessary to indicate the way something looks like it feels in a work (texture) or creating the repetition of shapes, lines or colors (patterns).

The optical illusions outlined in chapter four involve images that are sensed and perceived to be different from what they really are. An optical illusion causes the brain to see one thing or misinterpret what it sees when the image is actually something completely different. The images in an optical illusion are examples of how the mind and the eyes can play tricks on each other. These drawings can be confusing and sometimes dizzying to look at but are always fun to create. Impossible objects are also explored; drawings that are possible to represent in two dimensions but are not geometrically possible to exist in the physical world.

The final chapter is all about drawing "cool stuff". This is a random selection of items that my students have wanted to learn how to draw or have shown interest in. Specific exercises are provided that offer step by step guidelines for drawing a variety of subjects. Each lesson starts with an easy-to-draw shape that will become the basic structure of the drawing. From there, each step adds elements to that structure, allowing the artist to build on their creation and make a more detailed image. Some tutorials have more steps than others but all have been made as simple as possible. All you need is paper, a pencil and an eraser and you are ready to draw cool stuff. Once the drawing is complete, it can be colored, shaded or designed in any way you like to make it original. Following these exercises is a great way to practice your craft and start seeing things in terms of simple shapes within a complex object.

When perusing these chapters, there are a few tips to follow for a successful end product:

• Try not to skip any of the steps provided in each tutorial. It might appear faster to do so, but it is far more frustrating, especially for the beginner. Please, follow the sequence in order to achieve the best result.

• Draw lightly. Once the basic outline is drawn out, then lines can be made darker and more permanent. With a lighter hand, erasing becomes easier and fewer papers are crumpled up and thrown away.

• Your artwork should not look exactly like the one in the book. Try to make your work different from the images shown by adding "extra's" and more details. This makes each work of art unique and personal.

• If a drawing seems to be too difficult or you are spending too much time on it without success, step away from it for a bit. Taking breaks will allow you to come back to the work with a fresh perspective.

• Try blocking out the areas of the tutorial that you are not currently working on. After one step is finished, uncover the next step and draw what you see. By blocking out the steps you are not working on, the artwork becomes less challenging to attempt. Continue uncovering each step one by one and adding to your artwork until it is complete. It is a simple tactic but it works by getting you to focus on just one action at a time.

• With a bit of time and effort, you can do this. Creating art is a process and you should not expect your drawing to be instantly amazing. Start off with the first step and build on it from there. Anything worth doing takes time – so take your time! Patience is necessary. Don't rush and practice patience. Look at your artwork and figure out the lines that work and the lines that don't. Change them as needed.

"How to Draw Cool Stuff" can help to guide you through the creative thought process and provide plenty of ideas to get you started, but don't limit yourself to the confines of the book. Check out the lessons offered and take what you like from them. There are millions of cool things to draw out there and only a sampling are within these pages. The best cool stuff can be found in your imagination!

Chapter 1

The Basics

THE BASICS

Shapes and forms are a part of the world around us and are important elements of art. Notice various types of shapes in the natural world, both geometric and organic.

Shapes and forms are found in nature and are also used in the compositions of paintings and sculptures. The basic geometric shapes used in art are referred to as two-dimensional or 2D; having only width and height but no appearance of depth. Forms are referred to as three-dimensional or 3D; having the appearance of width, height and depth. There are also organic shapes seen in artworks (also known as free form or biomorphic shapes) that are frequently found in nature and do not have formal names.

A square is a two-dimensional (2D) shape that can be made into the three-dimensional (3D) form of a cube. A circle is a round, 2D shape in which every point on the outside is the same distance from the center. This can be made into the 3D form of a sphere that is shaped like a ball and circular from all possible points of view. The cone is a form that appears triangular at the tip yet round at the base, a 3D form having a surface created by a straight line (the side length) that tapers smoothly from a base to a point called the apex or vertex. The fourth basic form is the cylinder, a 3D geometric tube utilizing line and ellipse.

This chapter focuses on taking basic 2D shapes and drawing them so that they appear as 3D forms, the main forms seen within any drawing.

All forms, regardless of complexity, contain one or a combination of basic shapes. The four basic forms: Cube, Sphere, Cone and Cylinder and their construction are explored.

Creating objects using basic forms simplifies the process of drawing and makes it easier to see what shapes make up that object. By drawing forms as part of an object, the artist is able to show depth as well as height and width.

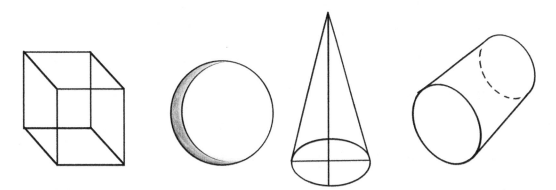

Shadows added to these forms make them appear more realistic and three dimensional. Blending, contrast, highlights, shading, shadows, and uses of value scale are revisited in order to review the need for these three dimensional qualities when drawing realistically.

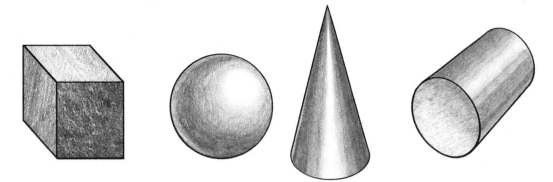

Once shading and light sources are reviewed, forms can then be turned into recognizable objects. Shapes and forms can be seen in almost every object imaginable. Although an object may not perfectly duplicate a specific form, these basic forms are present in some manner. There are millions of objects that have forms present within them. The samples shown in "The Basics" chapter have forms present within them and are offered only as a quick review to show the possibilities a form has to offer within an artwork.

At the end of the chapter you will find a few exercises that review the basic construction of a generic human form. This chapter is short but very important when learning how to construct a basic outline for anything that you draw. With a bit of practice drawing and observing objects around you, soon you will be identifying simple shapes and forms within objects and arranging them intuitively to create original works of art.

A BASIC CUBE

KNOW:
A 3D cube (form) can be drawn from a 2D square (shape)

UNDERSTAND:
• Perspective
• The variety of ways to draw a 3D cube

DO:
Students will practice drawing basic cubes.

VOCABULARY:

Cube – A symmetrical, three-dimensional shape contained by six equal squares.

Overlap - When one thing lies over and partly covers something else.

Parallel Lines - Two lines on a plane that never meet.

Perspective – The technique used to create the illusion of 3D onto a 2D surface. Perspective helps to create a sense of depth or receding space.

A Basic Cube

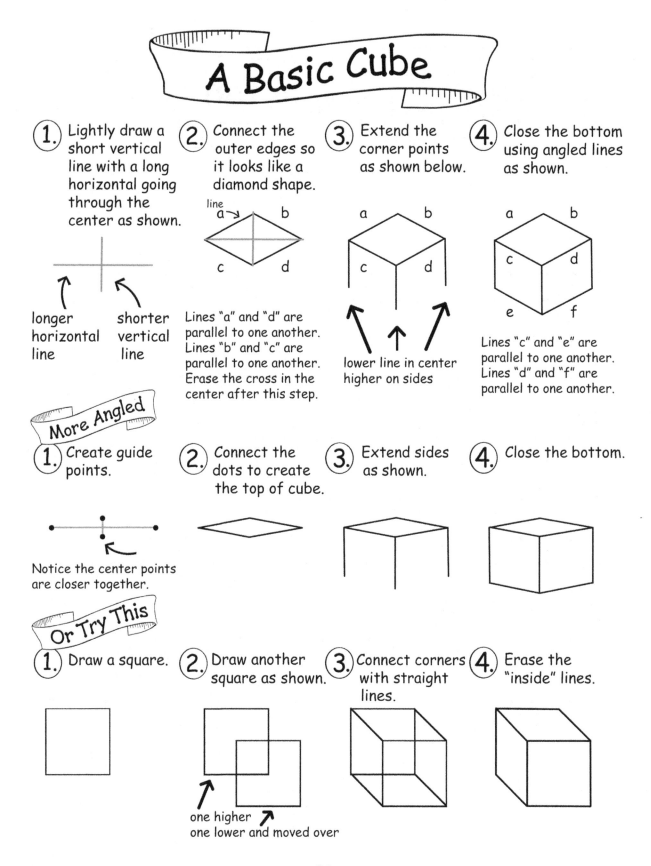

1. Lightly draw a short vertical line with a long horizontal going through the center as shown.

longer horizontal line

shorter vertical line

2. Connect the outer edges so it looks like a diamond shape.

line
a → b
c d

Lines "a" and "d" are parallel to one another. Lines "b" and "c" are parallel to one another. Erase the cross in the center after this step.

3. Extend the corner points as shown below.

a b
c d

lower line in center higher on sides

4. Close the bottom using angled lines as shown.

a b
c d
e f

Lines "c" and "e" are parallel to one another. Lines "d" and "f" are parallel to one another.

More Angled

1. Create guide points.

Notice the center points are closer together.

2. Connect the dots to create the top of cube.

3. Extend sides as shown.

4. Close the bottom.

Or Try This

1. Draw a square.

2. Draw another square as shown.

one higher
one lower and moved over

3. Connect corners with straight lines.

4. Erase the "inside" lines.

21

BASIC CONE

KNOW:
Cone, Ellipse, Perspective, Vertical

UNDERSTAND:
• The cone is one of the four basic forms that appears in nature and in man-made objects.
• There are several ways to draw a realistic looking cone.

DO:
Students will practice the variety of methods shown to create a cone.

TIPS:
• Start with a vertical line to establish the center of the cone.
• Next, construct a triangle using that vertical line which will bisect the triangle into two even halves.
• Attach an ellipse to the base of the triangle.

VOCABULARY:

Cone – A three-dimensional form having a surface created by a straight line (the side length) that tapers smoothly from a base to a point called the apex or vertex.

Ellipse – A circle viewed at an angle; an oval.

Perspective – The technique artists use to project an illusion of the three-dimensional world onto a two-dimensional surface. Perspective helps to create a sense of depth or receding space.

Vertical - The direction going straight up and down; the opposite of (or perpendicular to) horizontal. Any orientation neither vertical nor horizontal is diagonal.

Basic Cone

Try this . . .

1. Start with a long vertical line with a short horizontal at the bottom as shown.

2. Draw an ellipse at the bottom to indicate the base of the cone.

3. Connect the top of the vertical line to each edge of the ellipse.

4. Erase all of the guidelines drawn in step 1.

or this . . .

1. Start with a long vertical and short horizontal.

2. Connect the top of the vertical to the base as shown.

3. Draw a small line at the bottom and one inside as shown.

4. Use guides drawn in step 3 to create an ellipse.

5. Erase inside guides.

BASIC CYLINDER

KNOW:
Cylinder, Ellipse, Parallel, Perspective

UNDERSTAND:
• A cylinder is a circle that is projected into 3 dimensions. If you are looking directly at the top or bottom of a cylinder, all that is seen is a circle. The cylinder appears when viewing it askew or from the side.
• There are several ways to draw a realistic looking cylinder.
• Vertical cylinders will have parallel lines, non-vertical cylinders can utilize one point perspective.

DO:
Students will practice the variety of methods shown to practice drawing cylinders.

VOCABULARY:

Cylinder – A three-dimensional geometric form utilizing line and ellipse.
Ellipse – A circle viewed at an angle; an oval.
Parallel – Two or more straight lines or edges on the same plane that do not intersect. Parallel lines have the same direction.
Perspective – The technique artists use to project an illusion of the three-dimensional world onto a two-dimensional surface. Perspective helps to create a sense of depth or receding space.

Basic Cylinder

Short Cylinder

1. Start with two points.

point ↓ •   point ↓ •

2. Connect the points with rounded lines to make a thin oval.

3. Add 2 vertical lines directed straight down from both points.

4. Connect the base with a curved line.

↑ curve it!

Long Cylinder

1. Start with two points.

point ↓ •   point ↓ •

2. Connect the points with rounded lines to make a thin oval.

3. Add 2 long vertical lines coming straight down from each point.

4. Connect the base with a curved line.

↑ curve it!

Stacked Cylinders

1. Start with a basic cylinder & add a point to both sides as shown for a guide.

point ↓ •   point ↓ •

↑ curve it!

2. Connect the points with rounded lines to make a thin oval.

erase dotted areas "behind" the first cylinder

3. Add 2 long vertical lines coming straight down from each point.

4. Connect the base with a curved line.

continue as desired . . .

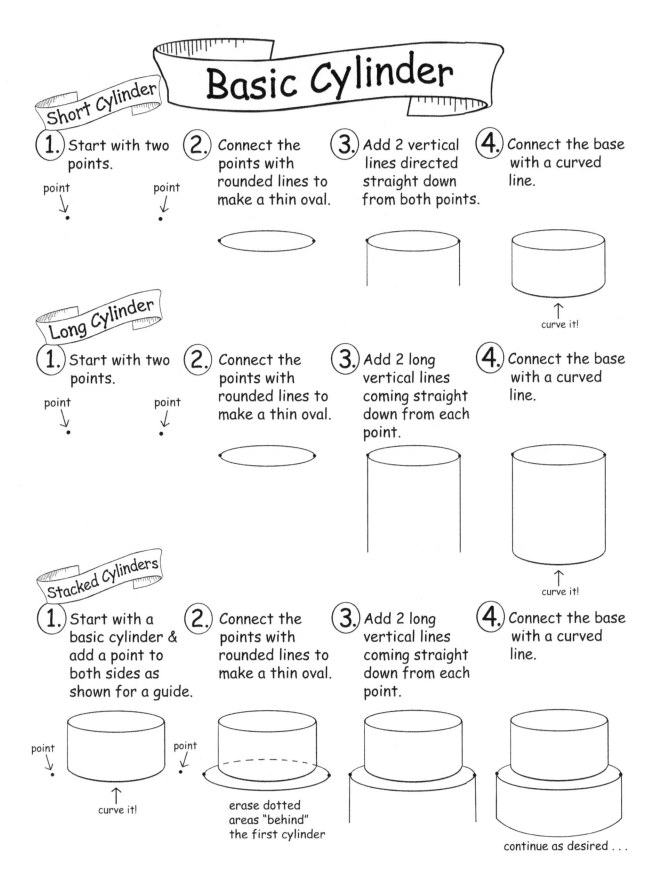

Basic Cylinder 2

Vertical

1. Start with a vertical line with a short horizontal at top and bottom as shown.

2. Draw an ellipse balanced equally at the top and bottom lines as shown.

3. Erase all lines drawn in step 1. These are only guidelines.

4. Connect top and bottom ellipses using horizontal lines.

erase dotted areas

Non-Vertical

1. Start with two ellipse shapes: a large one in front and a slightly smaller one above and to the right of the first.

2. Connect the two ellipses with angled lines as seen below.

3. Erase the in-side of the ellipse on the right (dotted area).

4. Final result should look similar to the cylinder below.

BASIC SPHERE

KNOW:
Circle, Light Source, Shading, Sphere

UNDERSTAND:
• Learning how to draw simple, three dimensional shapes like cubes and spheres is great practice for artists looking to hone their technical drawing skills.
• When shading, the darkest area of a sphere is furthest from the light source.
• The lightest area can be erased to create a highlight.

DO:
Students will practice drawing basic spheres using learned shading and blending techniques.

NOTES:
• As you shade towards the light source, use less and less pressure with the pencil. This means pressing heavier on the dark areas and lighter on the light areas.
• Indicate a direct light source so that deciding on dark areas and light ones will be easier.

VOCABULARY:

Circle – A round, two-dimensional shape in which every point on the outside is the same distance from the center.

Light Source – The direction from which light is coming from and shining on an object.

Reflected Light – When light bounces off of an object and is diffusely reflected; light that bounces back into a shaded area and modifies its tone.

Shading - Showing change from light to dark or dark to light in a picture.

Shadow - A dark area cast by an object illuminated on the opposite side.

Sphere - A three-dimensional form shaped like a ball, circular from all possible points of view. Its surface consists of points, all of which are the same distance (radius) from its center.

Basic Sphere

1. Draw the outline of a circle with a light, sketchy line. You can use a compass, trace a round object or try drawing it freehand.

2. Choose a direction that the light source will come from.

this lamp indicates the light source is coming from the upper right area

3. Start shading the area furthest from the light source. This will be the second darkest spot on the circle.

This slightly lighter area indicates reflected light

4. Shade toward the light source, adding a bit more pressure. This next shadow will be the darkest spot.

5. Fill the circle with less pressure as the shadow moves toward the light source. Leave a white area closest to the light source for a highlight.

6. Gently blend the shading and add a shadow below as shown. The circle shape will now appear as a spherical, 3D form.

Notice how the shadows are curved around the sphere form

SHADING FORMS

KNOW:
Blend, Contrast, Highlight, Shading, Shadows, Value Scale

UNDERSTAND:
• Value added to a shape (2D) when drawing creates form (3D).
• The lightness or darkness of a value can indicate where a light source falls on an object.
• Shading adds depth, contrast, character, and even movement to your drawings by capturing the shadows and highlights of your object.

DO:
Students will create a line drawing of each of the four basic forms (cube, sphere, cone and cylinder) and shade them using the value scale as a guideline.

NOTES:
• Observe the object and shade it in according to the value scale.
• Gently blending the light areas into the darker helps to create realistic shading.

VOCABULARY:

Blend – To mix marks or colors smoothly together on a surface. This is sometimes called feathering.

Contrast – A large difference between two things; for example, dark and light.

Highlight – The area on any surface which reflects the most light. Highlights and shadows are important to the achievement of realistic shading.

Shading - Showing change from light to dark or dark to light in a picture.

Shadow - A dark area cast by an object illuminated on the opposite side.

Value Scale - Values are the lights and darks of your drawing. A complete value scale will range from white all the way to black with many shades of gray in between.

Shading Forms

1. Value Scale

make a
rectangle
with 5
squares

number them: 1   2   3   4   5

Shade the squares

leave white	light gray	medium gray	dark gray	black
1	2	3	4	5

2. Flat Shading - CUBE

angle bottom

2
4
3
3

3. Round Shading - SPHERE

Add 3 more circles

highlight
mid-tone
shadow
reflected light

Shade

Blend

1
2
4
2

4. Cone

1.   2.   3.   4.   5.   6.

Shade   Blend

2   2
4   3   4
3   1

5. Cylinder

guide points

Shade   Blend

1 4 3 2 1 2 3 4 1

31

TURNING FORMS INTO OBJECTS

KNOW:
• The four basic forms: Cube, Sphere, Cone and Cylinder
• Blend, Contrast, Highlight, Shading, Shadows, Value Scale

UNDERSTAND:
• Value added to a shape (2D) when drawing creates form (3D).
• The lightness or darkness of a value can indicate where a light source falls on an object.
• Once you learn how to draw, overlap and shade the four basic forms in art, you will be able to combine them to draw most other forms.
• Most drawings and complex works of art can be broken down into basic shapes and forms.

DO: Students will utilize each of the four basic forms (cube, sphere, cone and cylinder) and turn them into a recognizable object and shade them in using shading and value scale.

NOTES: When drawing from life, observe the object you want to draw and determine what basic shapes/forms are needed to render the object.

VOCABULARY:
Cone – A three-dimensional shape having a surface formed by a straight line (the side length) that tapers smoothly from a base to a point called the apex or vertex.

Cube – A symmetrical three-dimensional shape, either solid or hollow, contained by six equal squares. A polyhedron having six square faces.

Cylinder – A three-dimensional geometric shape utilizing line and ellipse.

Sphere - A three-dimensional form shaped like a ball, circular from all possible points of view. Its surface consists of points, all of which are the same distance (radius) from its center.

Shading - Showing change from light to dark or dark to light in a picture.

Shadow - A dark area cast by an object illuminated on the opposite side.

Value Scale - Values are the lights and darks of your drawing. A complete value scale will range from white all the way to black with many shades of gray in between.

Forms Into Objects

1. Cube into a present

vertical | angle | horizontal | vertical

Start with a basic cube & draw ribbon lines.

Shade verticals lightly & angles darker.

Lightly shade top of cube. Side should be darker.

Add another shaded ribbon as shown.

Add a bow.

2. Sphere into a Globe

Start with a basic circle.

Add curved, vertical lines as shown. The center line is straight.

Add curved, horizontal lines as shown. The center line is straight.

Add continent shapes.

3. Cone into an Ice Cream

Start with a basic cone.

Curve lines in one direction

... then the other.

Draw an oval at the top.

Connect oval to cone.

use curved, cloud-like lines

Draw sprinkles.

Add a cherry.

4. Cylinder into a Fire-Cracker

don't use a ruler - curve lines a bit!

Draw cylinder at an angle.

Add a base.

Draw smaller oval inside top.

Add wick.

Add curved stripes.

Add sparks and shade.

HUMAN OUTLINE

KNOW:
• Simple shapes combined together can create more complex objects
• Layering, Overlapping
• Simple steps to create a realistic human figure

UNDERSTAND:
• Connecting simple shapes can be the first step to creating a basic human figure.
• The basics of proportion to create a realistic human outline.
• Features of the adult human body can be measured/created on a grid (7 heads tall).

DO:
Construct a proportionate human outline starting with an advanced stick figure with the basic head, torso, arms and legs then adding the width of shoulders and pelvis and the feet. Simplified forms of body parts can be added to the stick figure that focus on correct proportion, balance and pose. Finally, connect all of the body part shapes and erase the unnecessary lines inside to create a standard human body outline. Once this is done, the volumes can be exaggerated or changed to create a unique character.

NOTE:
You do not have to draw the "7 heads tall" guideline seen in step 1. That is just a sizing reference to indicate how much area will be needed to draw your figure.

VOCABULARY:

Layering – To place something over another surface or object.

Overlap - When one thing lies over, partly covering something else. Depicting this is one of the most important means of conveying an illusion of depth.

Proportion - The proportion relationship of one part to another in an object or the whole object with respect to size, quantity, degree or number.

Start with a basic stickman but add lines for shoulders, pelvis & feet

"The Candy Man"

Human Outline

Have a good eraser handy for this one!

1. Draw a stickman The average adult is "7 heads" tall.

2. Draw circle "M&M's" for shoulders, elbows, knees and ankles.

3. Add an oval ribcage and two overlapping gumball hips.

4. "Thicken" the arms and legs with tube-like licorice bites.

5. Draw ice cream cones for hands and feet.

add neck & erase dotted area

add rounded shoulders

cone shapes

cone shapes

6. Erase the lines inside the stickman.

erase all dotted areas

round toes

7. "Connect" the parts & erase inner shapes.

draw lines for chest detail

"Thicken" the middle, thighs, & and add calf muscles

8. Generic human outline.

rounded "mitten" hands

CVH

HUMAN OUTLINE VARIATIONS

KNOW:
• Simple shapes combined together can create more complex objects
• Layering, Overlapping
• Simple steps to create a realistic human figure

UNDERSTAND:
• Connecting simple shapes can be the first step to creating a basic human figure.
• Features of the adult human body can be measured/created on a grid (7 heads tall).
• Features of the child/baby human body can be measured/created on a grid (4-5 heads tall).
• Making shapes smaller or larger can be effective in creating a unique character.

DO: Construct a unique human outline using the tips and tricks provided. Simplified forms of body parts can be added to the stick figure that focus on correct proportion, balance and pose. Finally, connect all of the body part shapes and erase the unnecessary lines inside to create a standard human profile outline. Once this is done, the volumes can be exaggerated or changed to create a unique character. Notice the differences in size and shape for the individual characters highlighted in the tutorial.

VOCABULARY:

Anatomy – The study of body structure, whether human or animal, including the bones, the muscles, and all the other parts. Knowledge of anatomy is important when drawing and sculpting both human and animal figures.

Layering – To place something over another surface or object.

Overlap - When one thing lies over, partly covering something else. Depicting this is one of the most important means of conveying an illusion of depth.

Proportion - The proportion relationship of one part to another in an object or the whole object with respect to size, quantity, degree or number.

Don't forget . . . the average adult human is "7 heads" tall

Human Outline Variations

1. Muscular Man

- shoulders are wider
- neck is thicker
- connecting lines are rounded
- upper body is wider than lower
- rounded calf muscle

2. Feminine Form

- shoulders are closer together
- neck is leaner
- leaner arms and lower legs
- hips are wider

3. Tiny Tots

a.

baby

a.

child

b.

b.

a baby is approximately "4 heads" tall while an older child is "5 heads" tall

4. Plump Person

- shoulders are wider
- neck is thicker
- connecting lines are rounded
- belly area is the widest point
- rounded feet and hands

HUMAN PROFILE

KNOW:
• Profile
• Simple shapes combined together can create more complex objects
• Layering, Overlapping
• Simple steps to create a realistic human figure profile

UNDERSTAND:
• Connecting simple shapes can be the first step to creating a basic human figure.
• The basics of proportion to create a realistic human outline.
• Features of the adult human body can be measured/created on a grid (7 heads tall).

DO: Construct a proportionate human profile outline starting with the basic head, torso, arms and legs then adding the width of shoulders and pelvis and the feet. Simplified forms of body parts can be added to the stick figure that focus on correct proportion, balance and pose. Finally, connect all of the body part shapes and erase the unnecessary lines inside to create a standard human profile outline. Once this is done, the volumes can be exaggerated or changed to create a unique character.

NOTE: You do not have to draw the "7 heads tall" guideline seen in step 1. That is just a sizing reference to indicate how much area will be needed to draw your figure.

VOCABULARY:

Layering – To place something over another surface or object.

Overlap - When one thing lies over, partly covering something else. Depicting this is one of the most important means of conveying an illusion of depth.

Profile – A view of something from the side.

Proportion - The proportion relationship of one part to another in an object or the whole object with respect to size, quantity, degree or number.

No ruler needed. The straight lines are for guides only and will eventually be erased.

Human Profile

Have a good eraser handy for this one!

1. Draw a circle on a stick with feet.

Remember, the average adult is "7 heads" tall

2. Add circles for shoulders, elbows, knees and ankles.

Draw a small triangle for the chin area

Add a bent arm and circles for shoulder, elbow, knee and ankle joints

3. Add a rounded rib cage and a circle for the pelvis.

4. "Thicken" the arms and legs as shown.

Upper arm is thicker than forearm

Thigh area is thicker than lower leg

Bump for calf muscle

5. Erase lines inside the stickman.

Add cones for hands and feet

6. Connect neck and belly as shown.

Dent inward

Slightly rounded belly

7. "Connect" the body parts & erase guides.

8. Generic human outline.

Add nose bump and eyes

Add pectoral muscle detail

Round hand

Add 2nd leg

Round feet

39

Chapter 2

Shading

SHADING

Shading is one of the easiest ways to add depth, contrast, character and movement to your drawings. Shading captures the shadows and highlights within an image to help make artwork more realistic and interesting. There are several types of shading and many ways to go about doing it. This chapter will explain a few of these techniques.

This book was created to provide interesting and informative lessons without the need for expensive/multi-dimensional supplies: a regular pencil, paper and eraser are all that is needed for a successful drawing. The pencils marked with "HB", "2HB", or "2" are the regular, all-purpose pencils that are most common. These are the pencils that you are most likely to use in school or at work.

There are, however, specialized artist pencils available for complex shading projects. Specialized artist pencils come in two major graphite categories. These categories are labeled as "H" or "B" and they measure the hardness (H) or softness (B) of the marks made by the pencils' core. Along with the "B" or "H" letter grade, the graphite will also have a number next to that letter to indicate just how soft or hard a pencil mark is.

| 9H | 8H | 7H | 6H | 5H | 4H | 3H | 2H | H | F |

"H" Graphite Pencil Grading Scale

"H" stands for "hard" and refers to a hard graphite pencil. Hard pencils leave lighter, thinner marks and can sharpen to a very fine tip. These pencils are usually labeled with a number to indicate the degree of hardness followed by the letter H. Generally, the higher the number is, the lighter and thinner the mark will be. A 9H pencil will leave a mark that is much lighter and thinner than a 2H. Some scales will show an "F" grade between the "H" and the "HB". "F" often indicates "fine", "fine point" or "firm".

HB   B   2B   3B   4B   5B   6B   7B   8B   9B

"B" Graphite Pencil Grading Scale

"B" stands for "soft" and refers to a pencil that has soft graphite. Soft pencils leave darker, thicker, smudgy marks. These pencils are usually labeled with a number to indicate the degree of softness followed by the letter B. The higher the number, the softer and darker the mark will be. A 9B pencil will leave a mark that is much more smudgy and dark than a 2B. Softer pencils will dull faster than harder pencils and usually require more frequent sharpening. As you see by each chart, the scale goes up to 9 at each end, 9B being the softest to 9H being the hardest graphite. Both of these extreme ends of the scale are often too light or too dark for regular use.

Artists sometimes use a range of different pencil types in one drawing to render different effects. A hard pencil is often used for outlining or fine mechanical work while softer pencils, which allow for easy blending, are used for sketching and shading. Remember, these pencils are not necessary for you to be able to draw cool stuff. If only regular pencils are available – that is fine!

HB/2/2HB is by far the most common type of pencil out there and most likely the one you will use.

Before you begin shading, you will need a drawing of an object or scene to shade. Draw an outline of an object from real life, a photo or one of the images in this book that shows shading. Take your time and draw lightly. Drawing lightly allows the artist to erase any mistakes easily if needed. The outline of an image on paper is often referred to as **line art**. When sketching a drawing that will eventually be shaded, light outlines are best, not dark. Start with a light, sketchy outline and add more detail as the drawing progresses. Once all the lines look good to you, then they can be drawn darker and more permanent.

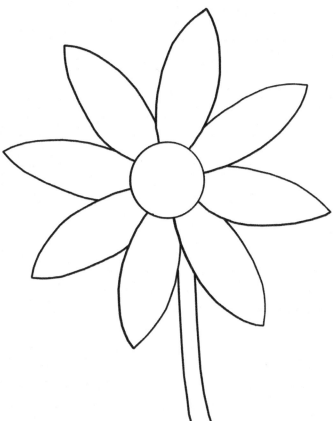

When drawing an item from life or a photo, look at the negative space around the object. **Negative space** is the area and spaces around the object that have no marks where as **positive space** is the area of the actual object or the area of interest. Basically, positive space is the space occupied by your subject while negative space is the space that is not your subject. The negative space in the drawing above is seen as white while the positive space is enclosed in black lines.

By paying attention to the negative space, an artist is more likely to draw an accurate representation of the object. People usually focus on the positive space in an artwork when drawing. As artists, we should pay attention to both positive and negative areas.

A **value scale** is a helpful tool to use when shading an artwork. A value scale, also known as a gray scale, is a series of spaces filled with the tints and shades of one color, starting with white or the lightest tint on one end, and gradually changing into the darkest shade or black on the other.

Special artist pencils are helpful but NOT needed to create a value scale. If using a regular pencil, press gently to get light shades and harder for darker shades. By controlling the pressure of the pencil, an artist can create a variety of shades.

| white | lightest gray | light gray | gray | dark gray | black |

Different pressures will leave different marks. Notice that the darkness intensifies as shades are filled in from left to right above. When used in artwork, a value scale translates into the light areas and dark areas in a drawing.

The above value scale was created by "coloring" with a back and forth motion using a regular pencil. This is a popular type of shading, especially when depth is needed in a pencil drawing. There can be hundreds of different gray tones between white and black. The value scale shown is just a small representation of the tones that can be created with your pencil.

Why is value needed in a realistic artwork? Value is a very important aspect in a drawing, perhaps even more important than color when it comes to the design and success of an artwork. Darkness and lightness are used to create a focal point within a painting or drawing. These are areas that a viewer immediately looks at. A light element against a dark element creates contrast that is pleasing to the eye. Not only does value create a focal point, it also offers a three-dimensional illusion of form to subject matter.

Other popular types of shading include **hatching, cross-hatching** and **stipple**. Hatching is the process of shading by using closely spaced parallel lines. This creates tonal effects of dark and light when the lines are placed close together or far apart, respectively. When more lines are placed at an angle across the first, usually in a perpendicular or near-perpendicular direction to the first set, it is called cross-hatching.

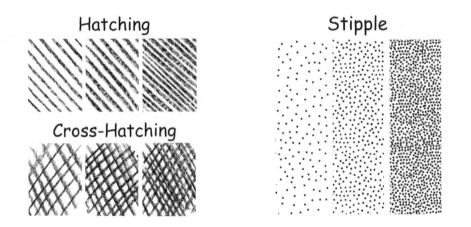

Hatching

Stipple

Cross-Hatching

Hatching and **cross hatching** are valuable tools for generating value and texture in a drawing and they work just as easily in both pencil or pen. Areas where hatching is put in a drawing will appear darker or to be in shadow. Areas without marks will appear as highlights. In the example above, all of the hatching is at a diagonal angle, however, hatching can be drawn at any angle. This method is one of the quickest and most effective ways to vary density and darken value in a drawing by creating a richer overall feel to a drawing. Cross-hatching can be applied as simple straight lines, just like parallel hatching, or it can follow the contours of the subject. When this method is done well, the close marks will appear to blend together from a distance.

Stipple is a method used in drawing, painting or engraving that uses dots rather than lines to create shading. This is a great way to add darkness quickly and easily while also adding texture. By "dotting" a pattern of points that are close together, the varying degrees of solidity in an object are represented.

The denser the dots, the darker the apparent shade. Stippling is mainly done in ink drawings, not pencil. The depth of tone and the roughness of texture can be changed by varying the density and distribution of the dots.

The best way to learn any of these techniques is to practice and experiment with them as often as you can.

SHADING STEP 1: Once a method of shading to use has been chosen, begin preliminary shading within the drawing. Lightly press down on the areas of the artwork that have the deepest shadows. This is just the beginning process so there is no need to draw too dark too quickly. By keeping the initial shading somewhat light, erasing areas of highlight or mistakes will be much simpler. In the preliminary shading done below, just the tips of each petal, the outside of the round center and the right side of the stem have been lightly shaded. Just the right side has been darkened to indicate a potential light source on the left. When drawing an item from life or a photo, it is important to locate the direction in which the light is coming from since we will be shading away from the light source; the brightest (lightest) areas will be those closest to the light and the darkest areas will be the furthest away.

SHADING STEP 2: Once the first layer of shadows has been laid, the pencil marks should become darker and more detailed. Leaving the brightest parts of the drawing white, the middle gray tones can be added and the darker areas can be darkened further. Lines have been drawn along the length of each petal for texture and the tips have been darkened more. The edges of the petal surrounding the center circle have been darkened slightly and the center has been filled in to be the darkest area on the drawing. Small dots (or stipples) have been added to the eye of the flower for texture as well. As you are drawing or shading any object, look at the subject frequently and compare it with the drawing to see where the main shadows and reflections lie. Keep darkening the drawing with a thin layer of shade. The contrast between light and dark areas will become more clear and distinct.

SHADING STEP 3: Continue to darken the outer edges of each petal and use your value scale as a guide. This will help the tones remain consistent throughout the shading process. As the shading deepens, the original outline of the drawing should disappear. Objects in real life don't have a solid outline around them, simply a change in value. The same goes for a realistic drawing; don't darken the outline, darken the shadows.

Once all of the tones are laid down, an artist may choose to blend the tones together for a smooth appearance. Fingers, cotton swabs or blending stumps can be used for this step. This will smooth out any rough edges and make the shading more gradual and realistic. Just beware of making mud! Rubbing too much will cause all of those fine lines and contrasting shades to smudge together and become the same muddled, flat gray tone. This takes the depth away from a drawing and makes the work appear less detailed. For best results when shading with the finger rub technique, just smudge a little!

On the opposite spectrum, the very brightest parts of the drawing should stay white to create highlights or reflections. If blending was done on the drawing, chances are the lighter areas have become smudged with some residual blending. This is easily fixed by gently erasing those smudged areas. Glares and reflections tend to be the brightest parts of a subject so be sure to indicate these areas in the artwork.

TIPS:

• When drawing from a photo, consider converting it to gray scale to use as a reference (make a copy of it using a copy machine on the photo setting). This will help the artist realize accurate shading since the object will already be in black and white.

• Having a hard time determining the dark areas from the lighter ones? Squint your eyes and these areas will become more evident.

• Using heavy pressure with your pencil will leave dark lines as light pressure will leave light marks. A combination of both with a gradual transition from one to the other is one approach to realistic shading. Practice using different pencil pressures to create a variety of tones.

• Remember to be careful if you choose to smudge your artwork to create shading effects. When done properly, smudging can be a quick and effective way to add depth to an artwork, however, the technique of smudging an artwork with a finger to create shadows can blur some intricately drawn lines and ruin a beautiful drawing. A good rule of thumb, don't rub more than three swipes!

• If available, use different grades of pencils from hard (H) to soft (B). This can make drawing with value easier. By letting the pencils do some of the work, you won't have to press as hard with the pencil to achieve dark values. This also offers more control when adding light values.

Quick and Simple Shading

When shading an object without a specific light source, there are a few tips and tricks to use to quickly create shadows and depth.

There are more technical and detailed ways to shade an object, however, below are two methods that are quick and simple. Try them both!

Try this . . .

Start with a simple form.	Press hard to darken one side.	Press lighter to shade the center.	Press hard again to darken the oppposite side.	Darken the base and top area.

or this . . .

Start with a simple form.	Press lightly and evenly to fill entire form.	Go back and press hard to darken one side.	Darken the other side.	Darken the base and top area.

When shading quickly or from memory without a specific light source, it makes sense to have darker shaded areas at the bottom of the object and lighter areas near the top.

For example, even an organic blob has a top and a bottom.

Darken the areas underneath each blob curve.

Shade the remaining areas lighter.

Erase some areas near the very top of each curve for a highlight.

Another example can be seen in this bowl. . .

(1.)

Start with this basic bowl shape using a 1/2 oval and an ellipse. (Don't forget the inner "thickness" rim of the bowl.)

(2.)

Darken just the outer edges of the bowl using a curved motion. Follow the curve of the base.

(3.)

Shade the remaining areas of the bowl lightly until it is completely filled in.

(4.)

Darken each side of the inside area of the bowl and erase spots on the rim and centers as shown to create a highlight.

51

REMEMBER RIBBON

KNOW:
Curve, Line, Overlapping, Shading

UNDERSTAND:
• How to create an effective design using simple shapes.
• Simple shapes combined together can create more complex objects.
• Overlapping.
• How to create the illusion of depth and layers so that parts of a drawing appear to be in front of or behind other parts.

DO:
• Students will discuss examples of two-dimensional images which have near and far elements, focusing on how overlap and differences in size help to achieve an illusion of depth.
• Students will follow the steps in the handout to create the image of a "Remember Ribbon". The overlapping will indicate which parts of the ribbon appear to be on top (in front) and which parts appear to be on the bottom (behind).

VOCABULARY:

Blend – To mix marks or colors smoothly together on a surface. This is sometimes called feathering.

Curve – A line or edge that deviates from straightness in a smooth, continuous way or, something that has the shape of a curve, such as an arc.

Line Art – An image that consists of distinct straight and curved lines on a plain background without gradations in shade or color.

Overlap – When one thing lies over another and partially covers it. Depicting this is one of the most important means of conveying the illusion of depth in a drawing.

The pink ribbon is an international symbol of breast cancer awareness.

Remember Ribbon

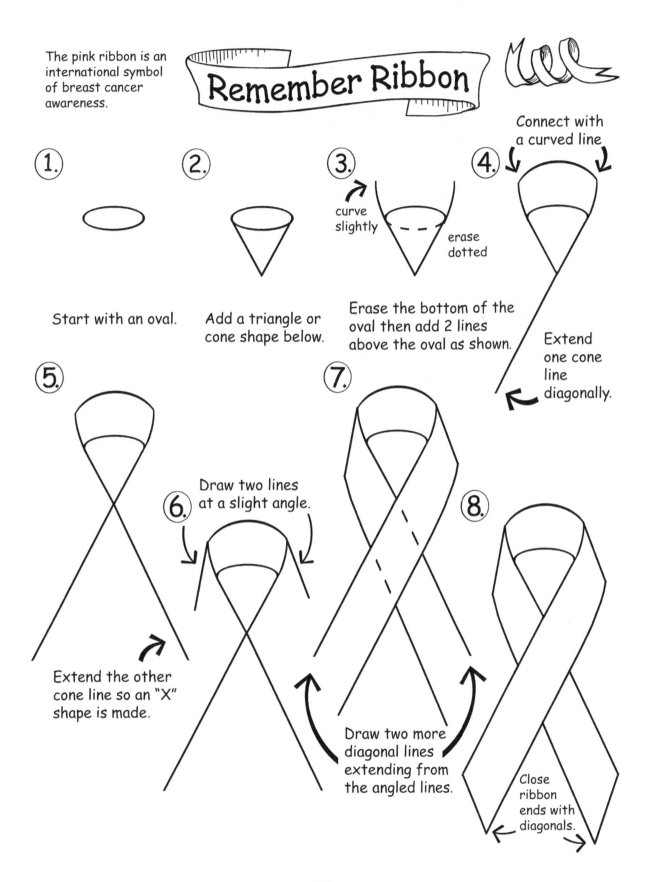

1. Start with an oval.

2. Add a triangle or cone shape below.

3. curve slightly — erase dotted — Erase the bottom of the oval then add 2 lines above the oval as shown.

4. Connect with a curved line — Extend one cone line diagonally.

5. Extend the other cone line so an "X" shape is made.

6. Draw two lines at a slight angle.

7. Draw two more diagonal lines extending from the angled lines.

8. Close ribbon ends with diagonals.

REMEMBER RIBBON WITH SHADING

KNOW:

Blend, Reflection, Shading

UNDERSTAND:

How to create the illusion of shadows and light in a drawing.

DO:

Students will follow the steps in the previous handout to create the image of a "Remember Ribbon" then start the shading process to capture the shadows and highlights in the ribbon. Follow the steps to gradually darken the ribbon, each time adding a thin layer of shade. The contrast between light areas and dark areas should become more clear and distinct after the completion of each step. This can be done with regular pencil for gray tones or with colored pencils.

VOCABULARY:

Blend – To mix marks or colors smoothly together on a surface. This is sometimes called feathering.

Reflection - An image given back by a reflecting surface, such as that of a mirror or still waters.

Shading - Showing change from light to dark or dark to light in a picture by darkening areas that would be shadowed and leaving other areas light. Blending of one value into another is sometimes called feathering. Shading is often used to produce illusions of dimension and depth.

Remember Ribbon with shading

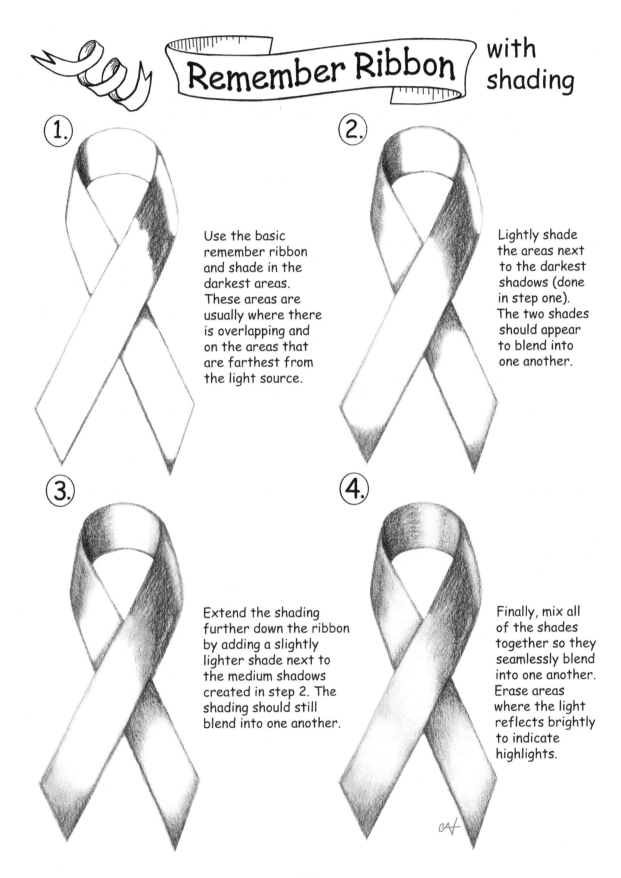

1. Use the basic remember ribbon and shade in the darkest areas. These areas are usually where there is overlapping and on the areas that are farthest from the light source.

2. Lightly shade the areas next to the darkest shadows (done in step one). The two shades should appear to blend into one another.

3. Extend the shading further down the ribbon by adding a slightly lighter shade next to the medium shadows created in step 2. The shading should still blend into one another.

4. Finally, mix all of the shades together so they seamlessly blend into one another. Erase areas where the light reflects brightly to indicate highlights.

SOAP BUBBLES

KNOW:
Curved Lines, Reflection, Shading, Sphere

UNDERSTAND:
Lines and shapes drawn in a curved manner on top of a circle shape help to create the illusion of a sphere.

DO:
• Create an original drawing of soap bubbles that appear 3D by "wrapping" the reflections and shading around the circle.
• Add details and shade.
• Draw several bubbles of varying sizes for a realistic effect.

VOCABULARY:

Overlap - When one thing lies over, partly covering something else. Depicting this is one of the most important means of conveying an illusion of depth.

Reflection - An image given back by a reflecting surface, such as that of a mirror or still waters.

Sphere – A three-dimensional ball form, circular from all points of view.

Soap Bubbles

What color is a bubble?

Simple Bubble

1. Lightly sketch a circle or trace a round object.
2. Draw two curved rectangles inside the circle.
3. Lightly shade inside contour of the circle.

leave a white rim

4. Gently smudge with finger.

clean up smudges outside of circle with an eraser

Detailed Bubble

1. Lightly sketch a circle or trace a round object.
2. Draw rounded lines that curve inside the bubble.
3. Lightly shade to connect lines as shown below.
4. Darken shading.

5. Connect with shading in the center.
6. Gently smudge with finger.
7. Add rounded rectangles and erase areas for highlights. Keep smudging and erasing until it looks good.

make many bubbles of varying sizes

shiny spots should be on the same spot of each bubble

SIMPLE SNAIL

KNOW:
Curve, Line Art, Spiral

UNDERSTAND:
• How to create an effective design using simple shapes.
• Simple shapes combined together can create more complex objects.

DO: Students will create a line drawing of a snail using simple shapes and curves.

NOTES:
• This tutorial shows how to create a neat spiral using a series of circles. Try this method and then try to free hand a spiral. See which one works best for you.
• Draw lightly so that the guidelines can easily be erased.

VOCABULARY:

Curve – A line or edge that deviates from straightness in a smooth, continuous way or, something that has the shape of a curve, such as an arc.

Line Art – An image that consists of distinct straight and curved lines on a plain background without gradations in shade or color.

Snail – A small gastropod mollusk animal that lives in a shell that it carries on its back, that moves very slowly, and that can live in water or on land.

Spiral – A line that winds or circles around a central point, usually getting closer to or farther away from that point.

spiral

Simple Snail

1. Start with a circle. Add a small crescent as shown.

2. Draw a circle inside the previous one. It should be off center in the lower left area.

3. Connect that smaller circle to the outer circle with a curve. Erase dotted area.

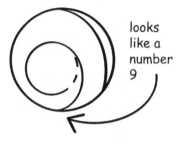

looks like a number 9

4. Add a smaller circle inside the middle circle as shown.

5. Connect small circle and middle circle with a curved line.

6. Add another small circle as shown. Erase dotted area.

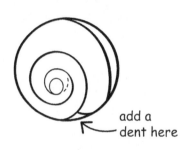

add a dent here

7. Draw one last tiny circle that touches the top of the last circle. Erase dotted area.

8. Add a rim to the front of the shell as shown.

9. Add body, head and eyestalks on the right and triangle tail on the left.

erase

SHADED SNAIL

KNOW: Blend, Combine, Curve, Value Scale

UNDERSTAND: Shading adds depth, contrast, character, and even movement to your drawings by capturing the shadows and highlights of your object.

DO: Students will create a line drawing using curves to create a spiral snail. Details and shading will be added using the tips and tricks provided.

NOTES:
• Typical school pencils are HB, which is a middle ground of hardness/softness. You can use an HB pencil if it is all you have available, but softer pencils (3B, 4B, 5B, etc.) will be easier to work with.
• Use light pencil lines so that they can be easily erased if needed.
• Pay special attention to any glares or reflections on the snail as those areas are the lightest areas. Leave the very brightest parts of the drawing white.
• When beginning the shading process, don't use the full darkness of the pencil so that areas can be erased or moved easily. This means press lightly and only sparingly fill in areas that need shading.
• Darken gradually, each time laying a thin layer of shade. The contrast between light areas and dark areas should become more clear and distinct.

VOCABULARY:
Blend – To mix marks or colors smoothly together on a surface. This is sometimes called feathering.

Curve – A line or edge that deviates from straightness in a smooth, continuous way or, something that has the shape of a curve, such as an arc.

Geometric Shape – A non-organic shape that utilizes rectilinear or simple curvilinear motifs or outlines in design.

Snail – A small gastropod mollusk animal that lives in a shell that it carries on its back, that moves very slowly, and that can live in water or on land.

Spiral – A line that winds or circles around a central point, usually getting closer to or farther away from that point.

Value Scale - Values are the lights and darks of your drawing. A complete value scale will range from white all the way to black with many shades of gray in between.

Shaded Snail

(1.) Start with a circle.

(2.) Add an overlapping oval on the left as shown.

(3.) Add another oval inside the top of the first as shown. Erase circle piece inside oval.

slight overlap

Draw a triangular curve here and extend it into the snail shell

(4.) Add a number 6 shape inside the small oval.

erase area indicated by dotted line

(5.) Continue the spiral inside the "6" shape in center.

connect with curve

(6.) Draw a curved body beneath the shell.

(7.) Draw head features then begin shading areas under spiral curves, under shell & under snail body.

(8.) Darken the shadows and add a shaded stripe at center. Add rim at lower body as shown.

(9.) Lightly shade the rest of the snail. Rub with finger to smudge if desired. Use eraser to highlight shiny spots.

CVH

61

A SIMPLE DAISY

KNOW:
• Simple shapes combined together can create more complex objects
• Simple steps to create a simple daisy
• Radial Balance, Repetition & Rotational Symmetry

UNDERSTAND:
• Connecting simple shapes can be the first step to creating a recognizable form
• A simple daisy is based on a circle with its design extending from (or focused upon) its center
• How to arrange elements in an artwork so that they appear symmetrical or equally balanced

DO:
• Follow the steps provided to create an original Simple Daisy design focusing on rotational symmetry.
• Shade with pencil or colored pencil.

VOCABULARY:

Balance - A principle of design, balance refers to the way the elements of art are arranged to create a feeling of stability in a work; a pleasing or harmonious arrangement or proportion of parts or areas in a design or composition.

Radial or Rotational Balance is any type of balance based on a circle with its design extending from or focused upon its center.

Rotational Symmetry - An object that looks the same after a certain amount of circular movement around that object's center.

Symmetry – An object that is the same on both sides.

A Simple Daisy

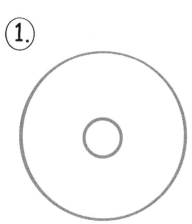

①.

Start by lightly drawing a big circle and add a smaller circle in the center for the "eye" of the flower.

TIP: try and find some circles to trace!

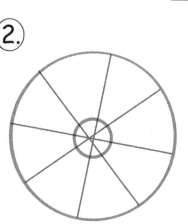

②.

Draw equally spaced lines crossing through the center of the small circle (looks like pizza slices). These lines will be guides for each petal.
It doesn't have to be perfect, just get it close.

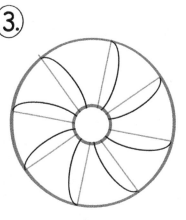

③.

Erase the marks inside the smaller circle then draw a curve as seen above next to each line. This will be 1/2 of each petal.

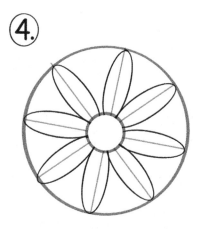

④.

Complete each petal with a curve on the opposite side of the center lines. The petals should look like long, lean ovals that are fanned out around the center circle.

⑤.

Erase the outer circle guideline, then draw long lines down the length of each petal as shown. Add texture to the center by adding dots.

continue to darken the outer edges of each petal

⑥.

Add a stem and shade it darker on one side and under the petal area. This creates the illusion of a rounded stem. Darken entire flower as desired.

GERBERA DAISY

KNOW:
• Simple shapes combined together can create more complex objects
• Steps to create a detailed Gerbera Daisy
• Layers, Overlapping, Repetition

UNDERSTAND:
• Connecting simple shapes is the first step to creating a recognizable, complex form.
• How to create the illusion of layers so that parts of a drawing appear to be in front of or behind other parts.

DO:
• Follow the steps provided to create an original Gerbera Daisy design.
• Be sure to follow the angles of each petal to indicate direction.
• Petals should be layered on top of one another for the illusion of 3D.
• Students will indicate which parts of their picture appear to be on "top" and which parts appear to be on the "bottom" using overlapping and size differences.
• Shade with pencil or colored pencil.

VOCABULARY:
Balance - A principle of design, balance refers to the way the elements of art are arranged to create a feeling of stability in a work; a pleasing or harmonious arrangement or proportion of parts or areas in a design or composition.

Layer – To place one thing on top of another; top layers will obscure bottom layers.

Overlap - When one thing lies over and partly covers something else.

Perspective – The technique used to create the illusion of 3D onto a 2D surface. Perspective helps to create a sense of depth or receding space.

Shading - Showing change from light to dark or dark to light in a picture by darkening areas that would be shadowed and leaving other areas light. Shading is often used to produce illusions of dimension and depth.

Gerbera Daisy

... more detailed than the simple daisy since it is viewed at an angle and includes shading ...

1. ⓐ

Draw a small oval for the center (eye).

ⓑ

Next, add a row of small petals (florets) curving around the top of the eye.

ⓒ ...

Do the same for the lower part of the eye.

2. ⓐ

Next, draw an array of petals under the eye. They should be short, stubby & slightly different lengths.

ⓑ

Next, add a layer of longer petals "under" those.

3. ⓐ

Draw a few smaller petals "underneath" & a few petals angled at the sides. Add three petals at the top.

ⓑ

4.
ⓐ

Add more petals around and "underneath" ...

ⓑ

5.

Finish by filling in the empty spaces with petals.

6.

Add the stem base with a curved line "behind" the petals.

7.

Start shading the petals that appear to be "underneath." Also, darken the areas around the eye as shown.

← Add a skinny stem

8.

Shade center of the petals as shown. Fill in the eye and darken the outer edges more.

9.

Continue shading. The closer the petal is to the eye, the darker the shading should be.

Shade stem darker on one side.

CVH

65

HORSE

KNOW:
Contour, Curve, Geometric Shapes, Overlap, Replicate

UNDERSTAND:
• How to create an effective likeness of an animal using simple shapes.
• Simple shapes combined together can create more complex objects.

DO:
Students will create a contour drawing of a horse using geometric shapes, curves and lines. Note the distance between shapes, the height of each shape and whether or not they overlap one another.

NOTES:
• This tutorial shows how to create an outline of a standing horse. The same basic geometric shapes can be used for a horse in motion.
• Draw lightly so that the guidelines can easily be erased. All areas marked with dashed lines are the spots to erase.

VOCABULARY:

Contour – The outline and other visible edges of a figure or object. A contour drawing uses contour lines to represent subject matter.

Curve – A line or edge that deviates from straightness in a smooth, continuous way or, something that has the shape of a curve, such as an arc.

Geometric Shape – Any shape or form having more mathematic than organic design. Geometric designs are typically made with straight lines or shapes from geometry.

Overlap – When one thing lies over, partly covering something else. Depicting this is one of the most important means of conveying an illusion of depth.

Replicate – To make a close copy of something; a replica.

Horse

1. Start with a long oval on one side for the horses chest and a circle shape on the other side for the rear. Leave a bit of space in between as shown.

2. Add two circles for the head and chin near the chest oval as shown.

higher

lower

3. Connect all of the circles as shown.

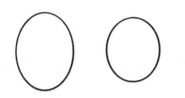

Two curved lines for the neck

Two lines to connect face

Connect chest & rear with two slightly curved lines

4. Erase areas indicated with dashed lines to form the contour of the horses body.

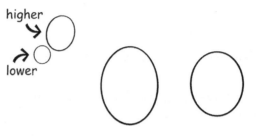

draw tiny connecting line here

5. Start the legs. Look closely at the shapes below the horse and try to replicate them.

Pay attention to which shapes overlap & which ones are higher or lower

6. Connect the leg joints to the body with curved lines as shown.

add ear shape

hoof detail: triangle tip with a curved base

SHADED HORSE

KNOW:
Blend, Contrast, Highlight, Value Scale

UNDERSTAND: Shading adds depth, contrast, character, and even movement to your drawings by capturing the shadows and highlights of your object.

DO: Students will create a line drawing of their subject using geometric shapes, curves and lines. Next, details will be added using shading and value scale.

NOTES:
• Observe the object that is being shaded and start by lightly outlining areas of darkness or shadow.
• Once the shaded areas have been outlined, lightly darken them, taking care to keep the lighter areas untouched.
• Gently blending the light areas into the darker helps to create realistic shading.

VOCABULARY:

Blend – To mix marks or colors smoothly together on a surface. This is sometimes called feathering.

Contrast – A large difference between two things; for example, dark and light.

Highlight – The area on any surface which reflects the most light. Highlights and shadows are important to the achievement of realistic shading.

Value Scale – Values are the lights and darks of your drawing. A complete value scale will range from white all the way to black with many shades of gray in between.

See previous page for horse outline drawing

Horse with Shading

shade using value scale

1. Add face details and erase dotted areas as shown below.

2. Lightly sketch the mane, tail and muscle areas. These areas are indicated by dark shadows on the horse body.

3. Add more shading to the underside of the horse. The upper area is usually lighter because of the light shining from above. Darken the tail as well.

4. Finalize the shading by darkening areas that are in shadow and erasing highlights on areas that should be light. This is contrast.

Blend as desired.

Notice highlights in mane, tail, rear, face and other rounder parts of the horse's body

SEAHORSE LINE ART

KNOW:
Contour, Curve, Geometric Shapes, Line, Scalloped Edge

UNDERSTAND:
• How to create an effective design using simple shapes.
• Simple shapes combined together can create more complex objects.
• Drawing in a light, sketchy manner makes objects easier to change or erase if needed.

DO:
Students will create a line drawing of their subject using geometric shapes, curves and scalloped edges to create an original seahorse creature.

VOCABULARY:

Contour – The outline and other visible edges of a figure or object. A contour drawing uses contour lines to represent subject matter.

Curve – A line or edge that deviates from straightness in a smooth, continuous way or, something that has the shape of a curve, such as an arc.

Geometric Shape – A non-organic shape that utilizes rectilinear or simple curvilinear motifs or outlines in design.

Line Art – An image that consists of distinct straight and curved lines on a plain background without gradations in shade or color.

Scalloped Edge – One of a series of similar curves that form a decorative edge or border on something.

Seahorses are a type of fish named for their equine (horse-like) appearance

Seahorse

1. Start with 3 circles.

← 1. medium sized tilted oval

← 2. larger oval-cicle

3. small circle off to the side →

2. Draw connecting lines as shown below.

curved line to connect head & body

← line for tail

3. Draw front of neck, front of tail & curve at small circle.

4. Connect tail and add snout.

erase dotted areas

5. Add small circle in tail.

erase dotted areas

6. Draw outer line to connect tail.

7. Add eye and back fin.

erase dotted areas

8. Add row of triangular fins around the back area.

9. Draw rectangle-like pattern on body.

add cheek fin

make scalloped edges

SEAHORSE WITH SHADING

KNOW:
Blend, Contrast, Curve, Geometric Shapes, Scalloped Edge, Value Scale

UNDERSTAND:
Shading adds depth, contrast, character, and even movement to your drawings by capturing the shadows and highlights of your object. Drawing in a light, sketchy manner makes objects easier to change or erase if needed.

DO: Students will create a line drawing of their subject using geometric shapes and value to create an original seahorse creature.

NOTES:
• Begin with a simple line drawing, add detail, then start the shading process.
• Shading adds depth, contrast, character and movement to an artwork by capturing the shadows and highlights of an object or scene.
• Darken gradually, each time laying a thin layer of shade. The contrast between light areas and dark areas should become more clear and distinct.
• Strong contrasts between light and dark in an artwork indicates bright highlights and deep shadows.

VOCABULARY:

Blend – To mix marks or colors smoothly together on a surface. This is sometimes called feathering.

Contrast – A large difference between two things; for example, hot and cold, green and red, light and shadow.

Curve – A line or edge that deviates from straightness in a smooth, continuous way or, something that has the shape of a curve, such as an arc.

Geometric Shape – A non-organic shape that utilizes rectilinear or simple curvilinear motifs or outlines in design.

Scalloped Edge – One of a series of similar curves that form a decorative edge or border on something.

Value Scale – Values are the lights and darks of your drawing. A complete value scale will range from white all the way to black with many shades of gray in between.

Seahorse with Shading

shade using value scale

1. Finish drawing all outline details including snout, eye & fin lines.

eyebrow
bag under eye
snout curves
cheek curves

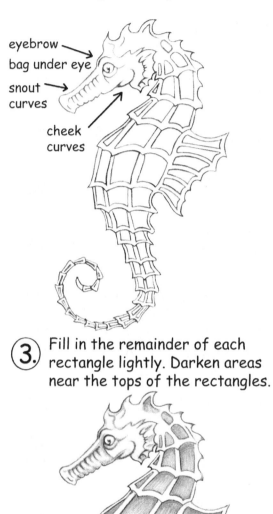

2. Lightly shade the tops of each curved rectangular shape, the snout and under the eye as seen below.

3. Fill in the remainder of each rectangle lightly. Darken areas near the tops of the rectangles.

4. Continue to darken certain areas to create an appealing contrast. Erase lightest areas for crisp highlights.

DANDELION

KNOW:

Balance, Blending, Layering Geometric Shapes, Rotational Balance

UNDERSTAND:
• Shading using value will achieve a more realistic rendering.
• The difference between shape and form.
• How to arrange elements in an artwork so that they appear symmetrical or equally balanced.
• How to create an effective design using simple shapes.
• Simple shapes combined together can create more complex objects.

DO: Follow the steps provided to create an original dandelion using the learned techniques which concentrate on overlapping, rotational symmetry and shading to convey the illusion of depth. Begin by drawing simple geometric shapes and connecting them to create a more complex, organic shape that resembles a flower. Add "Extras" like florets blowing away in the wind. Shade to indicate form. Erase areas for highlights.

VOCABULARY:

Balance – A principle of design, balance refers to the way the elements of art are arranged to create a feeling of stability in a work; a pleasing or harmonious arrangement or proportion of parts or areas in a design or composition.

Blending – To mix smoothly in order to obtain a particular style or look.

Floret – A small flower or one of the closely clustered small flowers that make up the flower head of a composite flower.

Geometric Shape – A non-organic shape that utilizes rectilinear or simple curvilinear motifs or outlines in design.

Radial or Rotational Balance is any type of balance based on a circle with its design extending from or focused upon its center.

Symmetry – (or symmetrical balance) - The parts of an image or object organized so that one side duplicates, or mirrors, the other.

Dandelion

1. Start with a wide oval. This will be the outer flower guideline. Add a smaller oval inside.

2. Connect a floret and seed as seen below to the center oval. This can be drawn as curved lines on a straight line.

floret

seed

3. Continue to draw the florets around the center oval using a rotational symmetry pattern.

Leave an empty area near top and bottom

4. Draw a triangular shaped base attached to the center oval with a long, thin stem.

5. Lightly shade the center oval and stem. Add another floret as shown (see arrow).

start a second row of florets & seeds under the first

6. Continue to draw a pattern of florets beneath the first row.

7. Finally, add a 3rd row of florets to fill the space.

8. Lightly smudge with a tissue or your finger to blend tones for a "fuzzy" look.

9. Draw a few random florets blowing in the wind.

A dandelion flower head is composed of hundreds of smaller florets (top) & seed heads (bottom)

CVH

75

SHADING WITH STIPPLING

KNOW:
Highlight, Pointillism, Stippling, Value Scale

UNDERSTAND: Stippling is a technique used to create images, light and shadow by making many small dots on a piece of paper that come together and appear as a blended form. This is a technique used by artists when shading with pen and ink which does not allow blending.

DO: Students will explore the process of stippling and how it can create the illusion of value in an artwork. Students will create a basic line drawing focusing only on the shape of an item then implement shading techniques using a series of dots known as stippling.

NOTES:
• Dots closer together appear to have a darker value while dots spread further apart offer a lighter value.

• When first practicing stipple techniques, have a photo or an object to look at as opposed to drawing from imagination. It is much easier to examine shadows and light as you draw by actually observing an object.

• Observe the light source and the direction of the light on the object. Light will determine what areas need more stippling and what areas need less.

• The smaller the mark that is made, the more realistic the image will look. Fine point pens are a great choice for this style of shading.

• An image with lots of dark values will need more stippling than an image with plenty of light. This means that the high density dots will require more time to recreate an image.

• Make dots – not dashes. Stipple carefully and always lift your pen completely off the paper before setting it back down.

• Try to keep all the dots evenly spaced.

• You do not have to stipple as directed in the tutorial: some artists cover their objects with widely-spaced dots first and then go back and add dark areas where needed. There is no right or wrong way to do it.

• Don't rush! Stippling can be time consuming. Step back and look at the drawing frequently from a distance. The dots should eventually look like a smooth, shaded image rather than just dots.

• When you feel comfortable, try drawing a color artwork using a form of stippling called "pointillism". Pointillism is a form of art made famous by the French artist George Seurat where dots of color are applied next to each other so that they appear to be blended together from a distance (visual mixing). For example: blue dots of paint or marker spread among yellow dots will appear green from a distance.

VOCABULARY:

Highlight – The area on any surface which reflects the most light. Highlights and shadows are important to the achievement of realistic shading.

Pointillism – A method of painting developed in France in the 1880s in which tiny dots of color are applied to a canvas. When viewed from a distance, the points of color appear to blend together to make other colors and to form shapes and outlines.

Stippling – Stipple is a drawing, painting or engraving method employing dots to make up an image rather than lines. These many dots are laid carefully side by side to indicate light and shadow. With this technique there is no line work since everything is comprised of dots.

Value Scale - Values are the lights and darks of your drawing. A complete value scale will range from white all the way to black with many shades of gray in between.

Stippling, a.k.a. pointillism, is a type of drawing that involves creating shapes & images via many small dots.

Shading with Stipple

1. Begin by sketching an outline of a simple image in PENCIL.

A fine pen works best for this type of shading. Use a pencil first to get the basic object outline. Start with pen at step 3.

2. It is helpful to outline the shapes of shadows seen on the object.

The lines seen on the pear at right indicate changes in shadow and tone. Draw these outlines lightly and in pencil as they will eventually be erased.

3. Begin stippling the darkest areas with a fine pen.

Carefully lift the pen and press it to the paper. The closer the dots are placed, the darker the area appears.

4. Stipple the next darkest area. Space this round of dots slightly further apart from those made in step 3.

Move slowly to avoid making dash lines.

5. Start filling in lighter areas with further spaced dots.

From far away, these dots will begin to appear as blended shadows.

6. Continue stippling lighter areas with fewer dots. Erase pencil lines when ink is dry.

Stippling can take a very long time to complete, so don't rush your work.

7. As shading continues, stippling should appear lighter as the dots are placed further apart.

8. Leave lightest area white to indicate a highlight.

9. Lastly, add more dots as needed so each area blends into one another.

Look at your art from a distance. The dots should come together & look like a shaded image rather than just dots.

78

TONAL VALUE PORTRAIT

KNOW:
Hatching and Cross-Hatching, Line

UNDERSTAND:
• Techniques used by draftsmen, engravers and other artists to shade when using mediums that do not allow blending.
• Hatching and cross-hatching is a method of line drawing that describes light and shadow. The representation of light utilizes the white or openness of the page, while shadow is created by a density of crossed lines.
• The density and movement of line indicate form by showing light and shadow.

DO: Practice hatching and cross-hatching by creating a value scale. Create a Tonal Value Portrait using learned techniques.

TIPS:
• Get a large photo or enlarge one on a photo copier so that is fills up a piece of paper (8.5"x 11"). Black and white works best. Even better: take the photo and "posterize" it using graphics software on a computer so the individual shades are easier to see.
• Take your time when outlining the features and again when numbering the shades. It may be a little time consuming and often downright confusing but it is worth it. The extra time you take now will take the guess work out of choosing what shade goes where.

VOCABULARY:
Hatching and Cross-Hatching - Creating tonal or shading effects with closely spaced parallel lines. When more such lines are placed at an angle across the first, it is called cross-hatching. Artists use this technique, varying the length, angle, closeness and other qualities of the lines, most commonly in drawing, linear painting, engraving, and ethnic art. Hatching is also referred to with the French word hachure.

Line - A mark with length and direction. An element of art which refers to the continuous mark made on some surface by a moving point.

TIP: If you can, "posterize" the photo using computer software. It breaks down the shades for you!

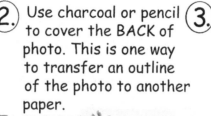

Tonal Value Portrait

using hatching and cross-hatching

1. Find a big, close-up photo of a face (or take one of yourself!) Make it black & white on photocopier.

2. Use charcoal or pencil to cover the BACK of photo. This is one way to transfer an outline of the photo to another paper.

3. Tape the photo to a different piece of paper (charcoal side DOWN). Use a pen or pencil to outline the major details.

↖ Take your time!

4. Gently separate the photo from the paper. The transfer drawing should look something like this.

5. Tape a clean piece of paper to the back of the PHOTO so your hands won't get dirty. Number the different shades directly on the PHOTO (not the drawing). Try to find a total of five different shades of gray.

Number everything that is white with a number 1.

Light Gray = 2

Gray = 3

Dark Gray = 4

Black = 5

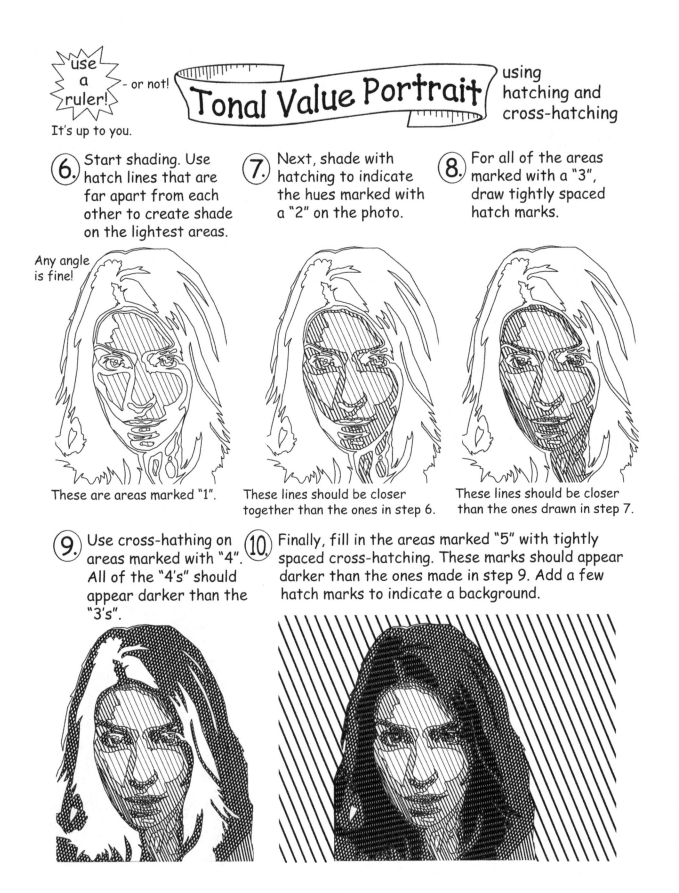

Tonal Value Portrait
using hatching and cross-hatching

6. Start shading. Use hatch lines that are far apart from each other to create shade on the lightest areas.

Any angle is fine!

These are areas marked "1".

7. Next, shade with hatching to indicate the hues marked with a "2" on the photo.

These lines should be closer together than the ones in step 6.

8. For all of the areas marked with a "3", draw tightly spaced hatch marks.

These lines should be closer than the ones drawn in step 7.

9. Use cross-hathing on areas marked with "4". All of the "4's" should appear darker than the "3's".

10. Finally, fill in the areas marked "5" with tightly spaced cross-hatching. These marks should appear darker than the ones made in step 9. Add a few hatch marks to indicate a background.

82

Tonal Value Portrait

using hatching and cross-hatching

Practice shading using
Hatching and Cross Hatching
Value Scale
Create examples of each in the spaces provided

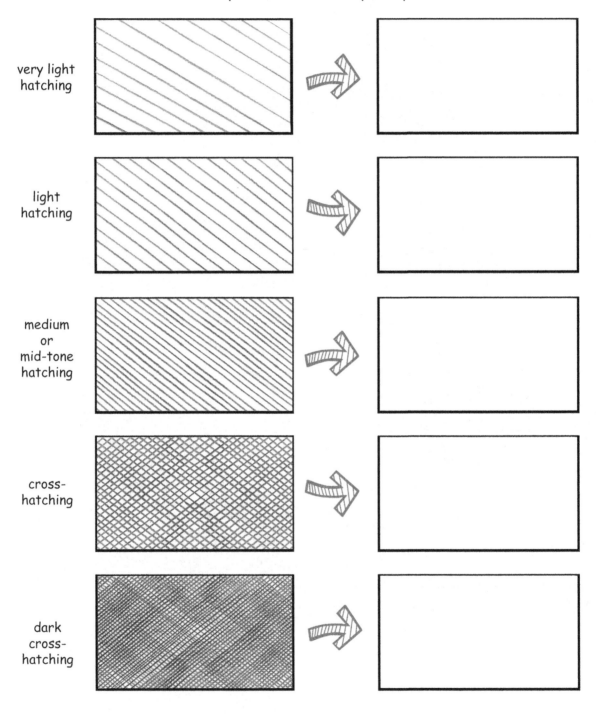

very light
hatching

light
hatching

medium
or
mid-tone
hatching

cross-
hatching

dark
cross-
hatching

Chapter 3

Texture & Pattern

TEXTURE AND PATTERN

Texture and pattern are two of the elements and principals of art that help to add interest and depth when used in a design.

Texture shows the surface quality or "feel" of an object; its smoothness, roughness, softness, etc. **Pattern** is the repetition of shapes, lines or colors.

What's the difference?

TEXTURE is the way something feels. In a drawing, texture is the way something *looks* like it feels.

| Furry Texture | Sandy Texture | Cracked Texture |

Textures are structures with irregular surface activity using lines and marks that are arranged randomly or without a specific pattern. Textures on objects are physical things that can be touched and felt. Textures can be smooth, rough, hard, soft, etc. In a drawing, that physical touch cannot be created, however, the perception of a physical quality can be created using *implied* texture. This visual texture is made by the artist through the use of line, shading and color.

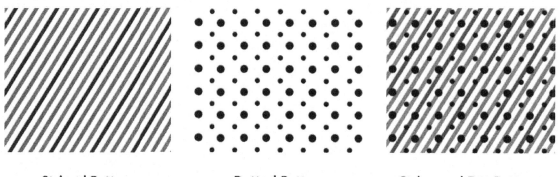

Striped Pattern   Dotted Pattern   Stripe and Dot Pattern

Patterns are shapes or objects that are repeated over and over again, usually structures with geometric or symmetrical qualities. Any kind of pattern in art refers to a theme or recurring visual event. Visual patterns are everywhere in both art and nature.

There are millions of textures and patterns that exist. Below is a small list of patterns and textures.

PATTERN IDEAS: Spirals, waves, bubbles, cracks, spots, stripes, curves, zig-zag, scales, checkerboard, floral, gingham, paisley, tweed, plaid, symmetrical or asymmetrical, barcode, basket weave, splatter, camouflage, rope, wood grain, lace, ombre, stipple, ripple, etc.

TEXTURE IDEAS: Flat, smooth, shiny, glossy, glittery, velvety, feathery, soft, wet, gooey, furry, sandy, leathery, crackled, prickly, abrasive, rough, furry, bumpy, corrugated, puffy, rusty, slimy, woven, woolen, flaky, etc.

TEXTURES and **PATTERNS** can be seen separately or can be combined together in one artwork. Below are two samples of both texture and pattern used together.

Tiger Stripe Pattern with Fur Texture   Rectangle Pattern with Brick Texture

The following exercises explore pattern and texture in design. Start with a simple warm-up of using a tracing of your hand to create a template to draw inside of. One lesson requires the repetition of a shape or object using a different pattern inside each finger. Another asks for the appearance of different surface qualities (textures) inside each finger. Have fun with this and don't be afraid to try out new patterns and textures that aren't listed or drawn.

Extension – Don't want to use a hand? Try drawing seasonal objects such as pumpkins in autumn or flowers with petals in spring that have separate sections. Add a different texture or pattern to each segment for the same practice.

FINGER PATTERNS

KNOW:
Pattern, Repetition

UNDERSTAND:
The elements of a pattern repeat in a predictable manner.

DO:
Students will practice creating the repetition of a design by tracing their hand and then drawing a pattern inside each finger.

NOTE: For best results, hold the pencil at a 90 degree angle when tracing the hand. This helps to create a realistic outline. There are millions of patterns to create – this worksheet shows only a few. Try creating your own original patterns for a unique artwork!

EXTRA CREDIT: Add a different pattern on the palm of the hand and another at the base of the hand on the "ground".

PATTERN IDEAS: Spirals, waves, bubbles, cracks, spots, stripes, curves, zig-zag, scales, checkerboard, floral, gingham, paisley, tweed, plaid, symmetrical or asymmetrical, bar-code, basket weave, splatter, camouflage, rope, wood grain, lace, ombre, stipple, ripple, etc.

VOCABULARY:

Non Representational Art – Another way to refer to Abstract Art. These artworks do not resemble, depict or portray any object or a thing in the natural world.

Pattern – The repetition of shapes, lines or colors.

Positive Space - Space in an artwork that is filled with something, such as lines, designs, color, or shapes.

Repetition – A way of combining elements of art so that the same elements are used over and over again.

Finger Patterns

A pattern is the repetition of shape, line or color
Practice creating patterns by filling each finger with a different design

Start by tracing your hand.

TIP: For best results, keep the pencil at a 90° angle.

There are millions of patterns you can create. These are just a few! Try copying the patterns shown or invent your own.

Dots

Scales

Diagonal
Circles on
Strings

Overlap
Weave

Stripes

"Wrap" the patterns around each finger for a 3D effect.

This checkerboard pattern appears 3D because it is "wrapped" around the wrist.

Look at your hand and draw the lines that you see to add detail.

FINGER TEXTURES

KNOW:
Repetition, Texture

UNDERSTAND:
• The techniques an artist uses to show how something might feel or what it is made of in an artwork.
• How to create the appearance of surface characteristics in an object.

DO:
Students will practice creating the illusion of tactile surface quality by tracing their hand and then filling each finger with a different texture.

NOTE:
For best results, hold the pencil at a 90 degree angle when tracing the hand. This helps to create a realistic outline. There are millions of textures that exist – this worksheet shows only a few. Try creating your own textures for a unique artwork!

EXTRA CREDIT: Add another texture on the palm of the hand and at the base of the hand on the "ground".

TEXTURE IDEAS: Flat, smooth, shiny, glossy, glittery, velvety, feathery, soft, wet, gooey, furry, sandy, leathery, crackled, prickly, abrasive, rough, furry, bumpy, corrugated, puffy, rusty, slimy, woven, woolen, flaky, etc.

VOCABULARY:

Repetition – A way of combining elements of art so that the same elements are used over and over again.

Tactile Textures – Refer to the immediate tangible feel of a surface (also known as physical texture).

Texture - The way something looks like it might feel like in an artwork. Simulated textures are suggested by an artist with different brushstrokes, pencil lines, etc. Texture describes either the way a three-dimensional work actually feels when touched, or the visual "feel" of a two-dimensional work.

Visual Textures - Refer to the visual impression that textures produce.

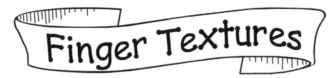

Finger Textures

Texture is the surface quality or "feel" of an object. In art, texture is the way something looks like it might feel. Simulated textures are suggested by an artist with different brushstrokes, pencil lines, etc.

Practice creating the illusion of physical texture by filling each finger with a different "feel."

Wooden Texture can be drawn as a bunch of long, curved lines going in the same direction with a knot here and there.

Wart Texture is made by drawing randomly spaced/sized bubbles.

Hairy Texture created using layers of lines.

Sand Texture created using a series of random dots.

Cracked Texture is created using connected lines of varying thicknesses.

Cracked Pedestal Texture created using zig-zag lines and cross-hatching.

There are millions of textures you can create - these are just a few! Try copying the textures shown or invent your own.

CVH

BRICK WALL

KNOW:
Parallel Lines, Pattern, Rectangle, Stagger

UNDERSTAND:
• The elements of a pattern repeat in a predictable manner.
• How to create the appearance of a brick wall by using staggering and pattern.

DO:
• Create a realistic pattern of a brick wall using the tips and tricks provided.
• Shade if desired (darker bricks/lighter areas between bricks).
• Erase some areas on each shaded brick to create a highlight effect.

VOCABULARY:

Parallel Lines - Two or more straight lines or edges on the same plane that do not intersect. Parallel lines have the same direction.

Pattern - The repetition of any thing including shapes, lines, or colors.

Rectangle – A four-sided shape that is made up of two pairs of parallel lines and that has four right angles. The shape has one pair of lines that is longer than the other pair.

Stagger – To arrange shapes in a series of different positions.

Brick Wall

Note: bricks used for creating walls are usually staggered for support

Simple Wall

1. Use a ruler and make a thin line at the top of the paper. This will be the first row of bricks.

2. Continue to fill paper with equally spaced lines.

row 1
row 2
row 3
row 4
row 5

3. Draw a rectangle in the upper left corner of row 1. Do the same for all of the odd numbered rows (1,3,5,7,9,11, etc.)

4. Continue to draw evenly spaced rectangles until each odd numbered row is filled.

5. Next, draw the same sized rectangle on row 2, placing it below the center of the 1st brick as shown.

6. Continue to draw rectangles using the same placement on all of the even numbered rows (2,4,6,8,10,12, etc.).

Detailed Wall

1. Follow step one above, leave a small space then draw another line. Continue to fill the paper this way.

This space indicates the cement that holds the bricks in place.

2. Fill with rectangles as seen in the steps above. Add a small space between each one as shown below.

3. Erase connecting lines between each brick. Shade bricks dark and the area between bricks light (or color).

95

CRACKS AND CLIFFS

KNOW:
Asymmetry, Depth, Pattern, Repetition, Texture

UNDERSTAND:
• The techniques an artist uses to show how something might feel or what it is made of in an artwork.
• How to create the appearance of surface characteristics in an object.
• The "Y" Trick (cracks look like the letter Y).

DO:
Students will:
• Practice creating the illusion of tactile surface quality.
• Follow the examples shown to create the illusion of surface cracks and edges of cliffs.
• Create the illusion of cracks using 'The "Y" Trick technique.

NOTE:
• Every crack is unique – no two are exactly alike. Cracks are usually asymmetrical.
• Drawings of cliffs should indicate towering height and depth. To help define the scale of a cliff, add objects beneath it such as trees or a river to show the cliff's size in relation to these other (smaller) natural formations.

VOCABULARY:

Asymmetry - Not identical on both sides of a central line; not symmetrical.

Depth - The third dimension. The apparent distance from front to back or near to far in an artwork.

Pattern – The repetition of shapes, lines or colors.

Repetition – A way of combining elements of art so that the same elements are used over and over again.

Texture - The way something looks like it might feel like in an artwork. Simulated textures are suggested by an artist with different brushstrokes, pencil lines, etc. Texture describes either the way a three-dimensional work actually feels when touched, or the visual "feel" of a two-dimensional work.

Visual Textures - Refers to the visual impression that textures produce.

Cracks and Cliffs

Draw a Crack Using the "Y" Trick

1. Start with a letter "Y" shape.

This should be drawn with shaky lines, not straight.

2. Add two letter "V's" to the tops of the "Y" shape as shown.

The "V" should be smaller than the "Y" opening.

3. Add four more "V's" to the top of the "V's" drawn in step 2.

Keep adding "V's" until your drawing looks like a cracked surface.

Drawing Cracks on Objects

Start with an outlined object.

Add a "V" shape on one edge.

Add a "Y" shape to that.

Add a small crack on opposite side

Take a chunk out.

Shade as desired.

Draw a Cliff

Start with the top of the cliff. Draw lots of jagged edges at the base.

Draw curved vertical lines from each edge.

Add more verticals coming from jagged edges as shown.

Draw things below cliff to show depth.

Hole in the Ground

using the "Y" trick, hatching and cross-hatching.

CVH

WEAVING DESIGN

KNOW:
Overlap, Pattern, Repetition, Texture, Weave

UNDERSTAND:
• Weaving is one of the most ancient forms of human creativity. Baskets and textiles would not have been possible without weaving.
• The simple over-under sequence that creates the illusion of a weaving within a drawing.
• The elements of a pattern repeat in a predictable manner.

DO: Students will practice creating the illusion of woven fabric by layering/overlapping thickened lines (ribbons) in the over-under sequence demonstrated in the tutorial. Students may use any length of ribbons as long as they use a minimum of five vertical and five horizontal ribbons in their design.

NOTE: For best results, don't use a ruler! Uneven edges and jagged lines look more authentic than straight, perfect lines in a weaving.

VOCABULARY:

Overlap – When one thing lies over, partly covering something else. Depicting this is one of the most important means of conveying an illusion of depth.

Repetition – A way of combining elements of art so that the same elements are used over and over again.

Pattern – The repetition of shapes, lines or colors.

Texture - The way something looks like it might feel like in an artwork. Simulated textures are suggested by an artist with different brushstrokes, pencil lines, etc. Texture describes either the way a three-dimensional work actually feels when touched, or the visual "feel" of a two-dimensional work.

Weaving - The interlacing of long, thin materials, such as yarn or thread to make cloth (fabric) or baskets.

This tutorial can be used to draw the likeness of woven material or as a template to actually weave something!

Weaving

NO ruler necessary

(actually, it looks better if the lines are hand-drawn and a bit crooked)

1. Draw a vertical ribbon and a horizontal ribbon overlapping as shown.

top ribbon is "over"
bottom ribbon is "under"

2. Add all of the horizontal ribbons.

(every other ribbon will be "under")

under
over
under
over
under
over

Dotted lines indicate "under".

3. Add another vertical ribbon.

Dotted indicates "under".

4. Add another vertical.

Erase dotted areas.

5. Keep adding verticals.

6. Shade.

CVH

MANDALAS

KNOW:
Elements and Principles of Design, Mandala, Radial and Symmetrical Balance, Radius, Circumference, Diameter, Compass, Template, Culture/Tradition

UNDERSTAND:
• Cultural, historical and personal use of mandalas.
• Circles are sacred symbols in some cultures.
• Art is done for a variety of purposes including ceremony, ritual, healing, meditation, joy and expression.

DO: Create an original mandala showing radial or symmetrical balance while including (and identifying) at least two elements of art, two principles of design, and at least three sections of an original pattern that radiates from the center of the work.

TIPS:

• Any shape or design can be used to create a mandala.

• Repeat the pattern. Each shape or design drawn in one section must be repeated in all sections. This is a key element in creating mandalas. Color must also be the same.

• Try not to over-analyze what shapes will be a part of the mandala. Select color and draw shapes and images based on what makes you feel good or what inspires you.

• Mandalas can have geometric shapes, organic forms or recognizable images. To personalize a mandala and add significance for the person creating it, add images that have personal meaning.

• Drawing/coloring a mandala can be a highly enriching experience in which you look inside yourself and find shapes, colors and patterns to represent anything meaningful. Mandalas are great tools for meditation and increasing self-awareness. Work in a quiet space (or with meditative music) and focus on every line drawn and every color laid down for the ultimate meditative experience.

• The best thing about designing your own mandala is that you have the freedom to choose whatever shapes and colors that you feel express your sense of self and your view of reality. This will help you to create a mandala drawing that is uniquely you.

• As more designs are added, the mandala will start to look more complex. Add more designs in empty spaces for a detailed artwork.

VOCABULARY:

Balance - A principle of design, balance refers to the way the elements of art are arranged to create a feeling of stability in a work; a pleasing or harmonious arrangement or proportion of parts or areas in a design or composition.

Circumference – The distance around a circle.

Diameter - A straight line segment that passes through the center of the circle and whose endpoints lie on the circle. Half of the diameter is the radius.

Elements of Design - The basic components used by the artist when producing works of art. Those elements are color, value, line, shape, form, texture, and space. The elements of art are among the literal qualities found in any artwork.

Mandala - Sanskrit word that means "circle". A mandala is a complex abstract design that is usually circular in form. Mandalas generally have one identifiable center point, from which emanates an array of symbols, shapes and forms.

Principles of Design - Describe the ways that artists use the elements of art in a work of art. Balance, emphasis, movement, pattern, repetition, proportion, rhythm, variety and unity.

Radial Balance - Design within a circle extending from or focused upon its center.

Repetition - Combining elements of art so that the same elements are used over and over again. Thus, a certain color or shape might be used several times in the same picture.

Rotational Symmetry - An object that looks the same after a certain amount of circular movement around that object's center.

Essential Questions:
How does art help us to understand the lives of people of different times, places and cultures? How does knowing the contexts, histories and traditions of art forms help us to create works of art and design?

Notes:
• Mandalas have been used in Tibetan meditations, the rose windows of Gothic cathedrals, the Aztec calendar stone, and Navaho sand paintings. In the East, mandalas are used as a focusing device for meditation. Carl Jung used the mandala as an integrative and centering device in psychotherapy.

• A mandala is considered "A Sacred Circle." It is the focal point that symbolizes our spirit, which (like the circle) has no beginning or end. A circle represents wholeness or completion.

• Mandala art therapy & healing can be a great source of reflection on one's soul.

• Creating a mandala is not about a final product; it is about the journey of creation.

Draw steps 1-3 lightly so it is easier to erase later

Mandalas

Have a good eraser handy for this one!

1. Use a compass or find a large circle to trace. Fill up the paper with the circle.

2. For a Mandala using radial balance, divide the circle into equal "pizza slice" sections.

3. Next, add at least two more circles inside the outer circle to make more sections.

4. Begin the design. Draw an interesting shape in one of the innermost sections.

5. Repeat that same shape in all of the inside sections. If it's not perfect, that's OK!

6. Add a border of your choosing around the shapes you just made to frame the design.

7. Repeat another design in the next section . . .

8. Keep adding shapes until it is very detailed.

9. Erase the guidelines and color as desired.

These steps are only an example. Choose your OWN important items and symbols!

Mandalas
Personalized

1. List at least five items that are important to YOU. Next, try to draw a symbol to represent each of those things.

1. Family ♡
2. Kitty
3. Faith ✝
4. Art
5. The Ocean

2. Draw a circle with guidelines and begin to add your symbols. Start in the center.

3. Repeat that symbol in all of the inside sections. Add more detail if desired.

4. Add the next section of symbols all the way around.

5. Fill in empty areas if desired with shapes or other symbols.

6. Add the next section of symbols . . .

7. Keep adding symbols until the mandala looks full and very detailed.

8. Erase the guidelines and add more details.

9. Color or shade as desired.

Lightly trace this Mandala template on a separate piece of paper

NATURAL SPIDER WEB

KNOW:
Asymmetry, Radial Balance, Repetition, Starburst, Symmetry, Uneven

UNDERSTAND:
A spider web is based on a circle with its design extending from (or focused upon) its center. A web is often slightly uneven but still holds a repetitive pattern.

DO:
• Create an original natural spider web design based on radial balance using the tips and tricks provided.
• Add a spider and other "extra's".

NOTES:
A spider web is a device created by a spider out of proteinaceous spider silk extruded from its spinnerets. This can usually be seen as white in color. For a more realistic rendition, try this exercise using white pencil, pastel or chalk on black paper.

VOCABULARY:

Asymmetric - Not identical on both sides of a central line; not symmetrical.

Radial or Rotational Balance is any type of balance based on a circle with its design extending from or focused upon its center.

Repetition – The act of repeating. To complete a specific action or performance again.

Starburst – A pattern of lines or rays radiating from a central point.

Symmetry – (or symmetrical balance) - The parts of an image or object organized so that one side duplicates, or mirrors, the other.

Symmetry is among the ten classes of patterns.

Uneven – Irregular, varying or not uniform.

Natural Spider Web

1.
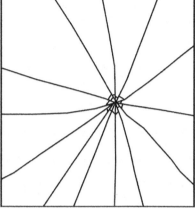

Start with a square shape. Draw an un-even starburst design inside.

2.

Near the center, draw lines across the starburst to create tiny, un-equal triangles (Looks like broken glass).

3.

Continue to add more lines coming from the center. It looks more realistic if the lines are a bit uneven.

4.
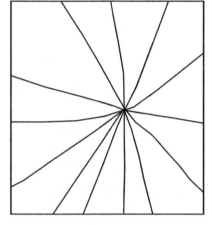

Keep adding layers of web radiating from the center.

5.
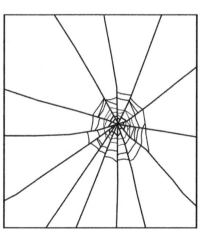

Continue to add web lines, each layer further apart from the last.

6.

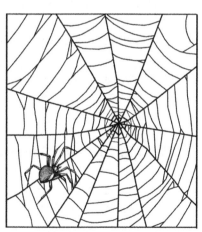

Finish the web using un-evenly spaced lines. Add a spider.
TIP: Spiders have eight legs!

DREAMCATCHER

KNOW:
Cultural Significance, Dreamcatcher, Symmetry, Weave

UNDERSTAND:
• In the Native American culture, the dreamcatcher is a well-known symbol that has deep rooted meanings and beliefs. Dreamcatchers originated with the Ojibwe people, who wove these magical webs from willow hoops and sinew. The hoop represents the travel of the sun and moon (giizis) through the sky. At night, the hole in the center only lets good dreams pass. Bad dreams are trapped in the web and dispelled at the first light of morning.
• Ancient traditions and beliefs can result in the creation of something beautiful and useful.
• All the parts of the dreamcatcher have meaning: the web represents the eternal web of life, weaving dreams and energy in the universe; the ring represents the earth and the circle of life; the beads on the web are blessings. The feathers represent a path for good dreams to slide down toward the dreamer while the wool of the webbing is a trap for bad dreams.
• How to arrange elements in an artwork so that they appear symmetrical or equally balanced.
• How to create an effective design using simple shapes.

DO: Follow the steps provided to create an original dreamcatcher design using the learned techniques which concentrate on overlapping, form and shading to convey the illusion of depth.

NOTES: The tutorial provides a guide for creating a dreamcatcher, however, there are many different ways to design one. The inside webbing does not have to have a particular pattern, just as the number of beads and feathers can vary. Use your imagination to create your own dreamcatcher design.

VOCABULARY:

Culture - The inherited ideas, beliefs, values and knowledge which constitute the shared ideas of a social group.

Dream Catcher - A Native American craftwork consisting of a small hoop covered with woven string, yarn or other fabric/material and decorated with feathers and beads. It is believed to give its owner good dreams.

Weaving - The interlacing of long, thin materials, such as yarn or thread to make a design, cloth (fabric) or baskets.

Repetition – The act of repeating. A repeated action, performance, production, or presentation.

Starburst – A pattern of lines or rays radiating from a central point.

Symmetry – (or symmetrical balance) - The parts of an image or object organized so that one side duplicates, or mirrors, the other.

Symmetry is among the ten classes of patterns.

Uneven – Irregular, varying or not uniform.

Dreamcatcher
page 1

1. Start with a tiny circle inside a larger circle.

2. Draw another circle inside the large one.

3. Next, draw 2 "petal" shapes surrounding the center circle.

4. Draw two more petals that overlap the first set as shown below.

5. Add two more . . .

6. . . . and two more . . .

7. . . . and two more . . .

8. . . . and one more!

9. Next, add curved lines around the outer ring for a "wrap" detail.

draw curves closer at 3, 6 9 & 12 o'clock

10. Draw feather outlines as shown below. These are angled so they appear to be blowing in the wind.

Feather TIP:

make a raindrop shape

↓

turn it upside-down and curve it

11. Add beads and a vein line curving through the center of each feather.

12. Add flowing ribbons to the feathers and draw a small circle for a "knot" to the inner woven areas.

draw a "knot" on areas that overlap

13. Add a hanging loop at top then shade if desired.

check out the angled lines on each feather for detail

CVH

112

DOODLING PATTERNS ON YOUR PAPER

Have you ever picked up a pen or pencil and began making designs or interesting marks on your paper while your teacher was lecturing in the classroom or your boss talking non-stop in the board room?

"Stop doodling!" is a common response to this seemingly mindless act of drawing. When someone is doodling, it looks like they aren't paying attention, are bored or are flat out being rude. Many believe that doodling is a distraction from the task at hand and hinders the learning process. After all, how can people be listening if they're decorating their papers with a maze of swirls, scribbles and checkerboard patterns? Teachers have been telling their students to stop doodling for years, however, contrary to popular belief, doodling has many benefits.

"Doodling" can appear to be an act done by someone not paying attention, but in fact it's quite the opposite! Doodling may actually help kids (and adults) to concentrate. Doodling is not a mindless activity. Instead, it engages the mind in a way that helps us think. Doodling is good for you!

Studies have shown that "sketching and doodling can improve our comprehension, creative thinking and attention span" (Andrade, 2009). This means that many people who doodle and sketch during an activity can actually remember more than non-doodlers. A person who doodles is absorbing information while they are doodling. The act of doodling during a lecture actually helps you retain more of what is being said aloud, reducing a person's need to daydream as they are forced to sit still and listen. Not only does it help one concentrate, it is a way of developing creative ideas. You don't need to be a great artist to doodle – you just need a little imagination. In fact, doodling can become great art, so doodle on.

References
Andrade, J. (2010), What does doodling do? Appl. Cognit. Psychol., 24: 100–106. doi: 10.1002/acp.1561

ZEN-DOODLES

Doodling can be a relaxing and fun way to create beautiful images by drawing simple patterns. This next section focuses on a form of making art based on the popular trend of creating miniature pieces of unplanned, abstract, black and white art. Zen-Doodles are beautiful, fun and relaxing to create. The word "Zen" reflects a high level of focus that incorporates the togetherness of body and mind offering enlightenment and relaxation. "Doodle" means to draw something without thinking about what you are doing. The process of creating a piece of Zen-Doodle art is a form of "artistic meditation." The creator can become completely engrossed in making each pattern, deliberately focusing on one mark at a time. Simply put, Zen-Doodles can be the process of drawing a complicated design by combining several simple patterns or designs together while the mind enters a focused, relaxed and meditative state.

The creativity options and pattern combinations are endless and anyone can do it. There are many benefits to doodling Zen-style as it provides artistic satisfaction along with exploring creativity and self-expression. It also provides a non-verbal outlet for entertainment, relaxation, problem solving skills, building confidence and improving hand/eye coordination – just to name a few.

This type of art is not intended to be a representation of something else. The doodle should be an unplanned, abstract, non-objective creation that grows organically as you make each deliberate stroke. The results should surprise you. In other words, you should have no idea what your completed artwork will look like before you begin. The creation will change many times as you add lines, patterns and designs to it. Zen-Doodles are usually spontaneous, self-paced and repetitive, however, there is no true formula as to what makes a good doodle. If you are relaxed, focused and drawing one line at a time, you are doing it right!

TIPS:

• There is no right side up or upside down – any way you hold the paper will look good.

• The work should be unplanned – the results should surprise you.

• The designs and patterns you draw should not represent anything in particular. Don't draw any numbers, letters or pictures. Your marks should not contain recognizable objects and should be a strictly non-representational design.

• Start small, preferably with a 3.5" square of paper. This will enable you to concentrate on a tiny area at a time and add a lot of detail to it without rushing or feeling overwhelmed.

• Leave at least a 1/4 inch margin around the edges of the paper that will act as a frame for your design.

• Use all the space at your disposal, but do not cram in the content - white space (negative space) can be an important part of the layout.

• Create contrast – certain areas should have more "weight" or thicker lines and shapes to create interest. Zen-Doodles with an equal balance of black and white shapes/designs are the most pleasing to the eye.

• Don't erase. Oftentimes, this type of drawing is done with a fine black pen (no pencil) so that every single mark made on the paper is used. It also reinforces the idea that one should not have a plan when doodling, just to let it happen. The artwork evolves after each mark is made.

• A pattern develops over time. When creating a pattern, many people just make a simple design and then leave it as is. They don't think to go back and add more. If you get stuck, try the following exercise: start with a line design. When that is completed, go back and add a line of squares (or some other shape) in between every other line. Then, go back again and add another shape or pattern inside the previous shape...continue this process until the space has been filled up in an interesting way. Take a step back from your artwork. Ask yourself: does the doodle appear balanced or is it too heavy with darkness or lightness on one side? A good Zen-Doodle will have an equal balance of positive and negative space. That means that the artist will need to fill in many areas with solid black or closely spaced lines, leaving other areas white.

• Notice that in many of the patterns provided, the details are very close together. There's not a lot of white space in between each design, line, or pattern. This makes the artwork look "fuller" and more interesting/detailed.

• Try to combine at least five different patterns together to create a one-of-a-kind artwork.

• The following pages show just a few of the millions of patterns you can create. These are only guidelines for you to follow and by no means your only choices. Use these ideas for inspiration if you feel stuck. The goal is to create your own Zen- Doodle.

• Most importantly, HAVE FUN!

Zen Doodle 1

1. Draw a border outlining the shape of the doodle. It is common to use a small square shape (about three inches wide) as most doodles are created in one sitting.

Add a thin (very light) margin on each side as a border.

2. Draw sections of strings. Strings are lines that divide the shape into individual sections.

Strings can be symmetrical or asymmetrical, curved or not: you decide!

3. Make some of the strings more bold to add contrast and interest.

4. Fill one section with a repetitive pattern. Don't spend too much time planning the pattern, just draw...

. . .the pattern will reveal itself as the drawing unfolds!

5. Repeat filling each section with a different pattern.

Focus on the patterns being drawn and pay attention to each line.

6. Continue filling in the strings until all areas are balanced or filled up. Make sure there is contrast.

Keep going until you are done! Erase the border from step 1.

Zen Doodle 2

1.

2.

3.

Draw a thin (very light) border outlining the shape of the doodle. It is common to use a square about 3" wide.

Instead of strings, draw a small shape or simple design inside.

Draw more shapes using different sizes and over-lap them them to create an interesting design.

Specifically Placed

1.

2.

3.

Draw a margin around the edges then add a small shape or design inside.

Repeat that design equal distances apart from one another to fill up space.

Connect the shapes with a combination of thick and thin lines to create interest. Keep going until it is done! Erase the inner margin when complete.

Zen Doodle

Pattern Ideas

Triangles within triangles

X weave with dots

Striped Scales

Bubbles

Crazy string

Random spirals

Geometric swirl

Piano key stripes

Leaf circle

Vine spiral

Circles and pin stripes

Connected circles

Zen Doodle

More Pattern Ideas

Basket weave

Plant Spiral

Waves

Contrasting circles & triangles

Stripes and dots

Ribbon weave

Rattlesnake tails

Connected google eyes

Braids and dots

Tubes and rings

Layered ovals

Flower power

Zen Doodle
Sample

ZEN DOODLE ANIMAL

KNOW:
Asymmetry, Balance, Pattern, Positive and Negative Space, Silhouette, Strings, Symmetry

UNDERSTAND:
• How to create a successful silhouette of a recognizable object.
• Zen Doodle Animals can utilize random patterns or follow the natural lines of the body.

DO: Students will create an original "Zen Doodle Animal" using a variety of patterns combined to make a unique design. The artist will start breaking up large sections into "strings" and eventually focus on small shapes, lines and designs within each string. Lastly, emphasis will be placed on the positive and negative space within the outlined canvas to create a pleasing, balanced design.

NOTES: The handouts are provided for ideas. Make up your <u>own</u> original, non-representational design/pattern that is different from the ones seen on the handout.

VOCABULARY:

Asymmetric - Not identical on both sides of a central line; not symmetrical.

Balance – The way the elements of art are arranged to create a feeling of stability in a work. A pleasing arrangement of parts in a design or composition.

Negative Space - Empty space in an artwork; a void.

Pattern – The repetition of any thing (shapes, lines, or colors) also called a motif, in a design.

Positive Space - Space in an artwork that is filled with something, such as lines, designs, color, or shapes.

Silhouette – A recognizable outline of an object.

Strings – A freeform shape or separation of an object into parts using lines or swirls. Intricate patterns are later drawn inside each string.

Symmetry – (or symmetrical balance) - The parts of an image or object organized so that one side duplicates, or mirrors, the other.

Symmetry is among the ten classes of patterns.

Zen Doodle Animal

Take your
Doodle to
the next level

1. Find or draw an outline (silhouette) of an animal, insect or other creature.

2. Draw strings inside. Strings are lines that divide the shape into individual sections.

Follow the natural shape of the animal or create a random pattern.

3. Fill a section with a pattern. Don't spend too much time planning it out, just draw . . .

. . . the design will reveal itself as the drawing unfolds!

4. Add a different pattern to another section.

5. Next, add yet another pattern to complete that section.

6. Look over the patterns you just made and add more details if needed.

7. Continue to fill each area with a different pattern.

8. Focus on the design & pay attention to each line drawn.

9. Fill with patterns until complete. Zen Animals can be symmetrical or asymmetrical.

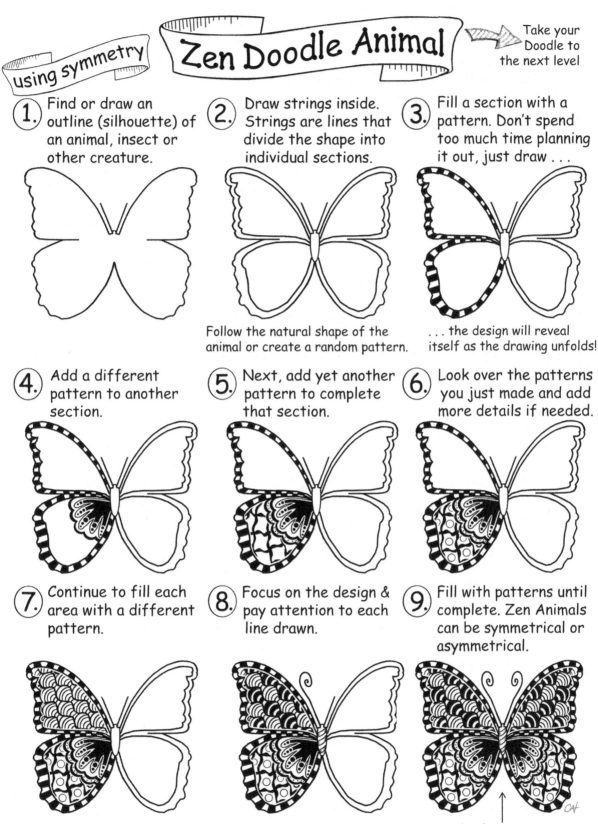

example of mirror symmetry

Zen Doodle Animal

1. Start with a silhouette of an animal, insect, etc.

2. Draw strings inside. The strings below follow the shape of the lion but yours don't have to. Strings can be more abstract.

3. Fill one section with a pattern. Concentrate & spend at least 10-15 minutes on this one section.

4. Draw a different pattern on another section.

5. Fill another area with another pattern.

6. Draw another design inside yet another string.

7. Take your time and continue to fill each area with a different pattern or design.

8. Make sure to add a a nice balance between black and white.

9. Keep drawing until the outline is filled.

Chapter 4

Optical Illusions

OPTICAL ILLUSIONS

Optical illusions involve images that are sensed and perceived to be different from what they really are. This causes the brain to see one thing or misinterpret what it sees when the image is actually something completely different. The images in an optical illusion are examples of how the mind and the eyes can play tricks on each other. These illusions can be confusing and sometimes dizzying to look at but are always fun to create.

There are three main types of optical illusions. The first is the literal optical illusion which shows an image that is different from what the actual image is. An example of this is an artwork made of many small objects placed together to create a larger object, portrait or scene.

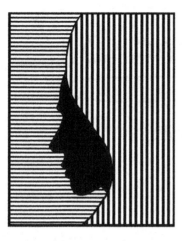

The second type of optical illusion is the physiological optical illusion. With this type of illusion, the brain presumes that the image is the result of an effect of excessive interaction or stimulation. The eyes and the brain are affected as a result of something happening with the color, contrast, size or movement within an image.

The third type of optical illusion is the cognitive illusion which refers to an image that affects unconscious inferences such as distortion of the image or human perception. These can include geometric optical illusions that present distortions of length, shape, size, curvature or position, ambiguous illusions which may have more than one interpretation or a double meaning, fictional illusions that elict perception of a figure that is not actually present in the image, or paradox illusions that appear to be improbable images.

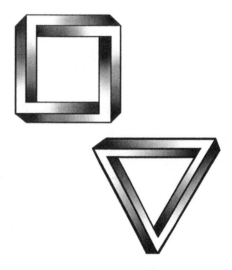

All optical illusions are made to trick the eye and make the viewer think they are looking at something they are actually not really seeing. They can use color, contrast, patterns, lines and shapes to create images that mislead our brains into creating a perception that does not match the true image. This happens as the brain tries to interpret information that is presented in a logical manner but the eye is sending a different message.

Check out the following pages for a sampling of how to draw a few cool optical illusions.

GEOMETRIC SHAPE ILLUSION

KNOW:
Geometric Shape, Illusion, Illusory Motion, Optical Art

UNDERSTAND:
• Op art, also known as optical art, is a style of visual art that makes use of optical illusions. Op artworks create an impression of movement on the picture surface. This is also known as Perceptual Abstraction.
• Optical Illusions can use color, light and patterns to create images that can be deceptive or misleading to our brains.
• Optical illusions occur because our brain is trying to interpret what we see and make sense of the world around us.
• Optical illusions simply trick our brains into seeing things which may or may not be real.

DO:
• Students will create simple, op-art patterns using parallel lines and geometric shapes to make an original optical illusion design using pattern and repetition.
• Students will then evaluate each space in the design to determine which color or shade (if any) needs to be in the pattern in order to create an optical illusion that shows movement.

VOCABULARY:

Geometric Shape – Any shape having more mathematic than organic design. These are typically made with straight lines or shapes from geometry, including circles, ovals, triangles, rectangles, squares, etc.

Illusion – A deceptive or misleading image or idea.

Illusory Motion - Also known as motion illusion, is an optical illusion in which a static image appears to be moving due to the cognitive effects of interacting color contrasts or shape position.

Op Art – An art style in which the impression of movement is created on the picture surface by means of optical illusion, also known as Optical Art or Perceptual Abstraction.

Parallel – Two or more straight lines or edges on the same plane that do not intersect. Parallel lines have the same direction.

Pattern – The repetition of shapes, lines or colors.

Geo-Illusion

1. Start by drawing a series of geometric shapes as shown. Placing them off center and at an angle adds interest.

Squares are used above, however, any single shape can be used successfully.

2. Draw lines through the corner points of each shape so an "X" is made in the smallest, center shape.

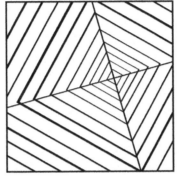

If the lines don't fall exactly on the corner points, that's OK. Just get it close.

3. Add two or three geometric shapes inside of the main design as seen below.

Notice the square, circle and triangle added on top of the existing design. Overlap these smaller shapes as desired.

4. Choose an area near the center of the design and start filling in every other block with a solid color.

No two blocks of color should touch if possible.

5. Continue filling in every other closed-in area using a checkerboard pattern. Pay close attention to which areas are being filled.

6. The final artwork will appear as an intricate geometric design that shows illusory motion.

FACE PROFILE ILLUSION

KNOW:
Line, Optical Illusion, Parallel, Pattern

UNDERSTAND:
• Repetition can create unity within a work of art.
• Close parallel lines can appear to create movement when used in optical illusion art.

DO:
• Students will identify repetition and variety of lines in a work of art.
• Students will use pattern to create a detailed optical illusion.
• Using the tips and tricks provided, students will use a series of horizontal, vertical and diagonal lines to create an interesting, unique artwork that indicates movement.

TIPS:
• Use a ruler!
• If using a ruler with marker, the marker can tend to smudge easily if the ruler is slid from one area to another without letting the ink dry. To avoid this, lift up the ruler and place it into position as opposed to sliding it into position.

VOCABULARY:
Line - Any line that is clearly drawn and marks direction.

Optical Illusion – An image that deceives a person, leading to a misinterpretation of its meaning.

Parallel – Two or more straight lines or edges on the same plane that do not intersect. Parallel lines have the same direction.

Pattern – The repetition of shapes, lines or colors.

Check out "Human Face Profile" in the "Cool Stuff" chapter for how to draw a face view from the side

Face Profile Illusion

Use a Ruler!
(to make the lines)

1. Start by drawing the "Human Face Profile" (as seen in this book) or draw one from memory. It may go off the page slightly.

2. Erase all of the inside details so only the profile silhouette remains.

3. Add an interesting curved line that covers most of the head. The main part of the face should not be covered.

4. Using a ruler and a thin marker or pen, draw a series of lean, horizontal lines in the area outside of the face. Be careful not to smudge!

Erase dotted area inside curve . . .

5. Using a ruler, draw a series of lean, vertical lines inside the "hair" area, leaving the face blank.

6. Color the face in solid or design a colorful pattern inside the blank area to create the feeling of movement.

MAN IN A BOX

KNOW:
Perspective, Optical Illusion, Differences between near and far objects in a scene

UNDERSTAND:
• The illusion of depth can be created using one point perspective techniques.
• When one point perspective is used, all lines appear to meet at a single point.
• Receding lines create straight edges that appear to go back into space.

DO:
• Create an original artwork using a vanishing point and receding lines.
• Following the techniques provided, create the illusion of the inside of a 3D room or box that appears larger at the outer opening and smaller as the lines recede toward the center. Shade and add a person (or creature or other item) in the back of the "box" to indicate the illusion of someone (something) at the "far" end of the room/box.

TIPS:
• Use a ruler!
• Draw lightly as the center lines and vanishing point inside of the smallest square will be erased.
• Shade the perspective boxes using a "checkerboard" pattern to create interest.

VOCABULARY:
Checkerboard – A pattern consisting of alternating dark and light squares, often black and white.

Line - Any line that is clearly drawn and marks direction.

One Point Perspective – A form of linear perspective in which all lines appear to meet at a single point on the horizon.

Receding lines – Lines that move back or away from the foreground.

Vanishing Point – A point on a horizon line where lines between near and distant objects appear to meet in order to produce an illusion of depth.

Man in a Box

Draw lightly . . . there will be a bit of erasing

1. Draw a large box with an "X" through it.

Ends of "X" touch each corner

2. Add a vanishing point in the center of "X".

Vanishing → point in center

3. Draw a small square inside the large one.

Corners touch each line of the "X"

4. Draw a cross inside the square as shown.

5. Draw another square inside the large one.

6. Find center of each section & mark a dot.

outer edges have 8 dots

7. Connect outer dots to center point as shown.

8. Fill remaining space in center with squares.

Erase middle

9. Shade checkerboard pattern and add man.

CVH

OP ART CUBE

KNOW:
Illusion, Op-Art, Parallel, Pattern

UNDERSTAND:
• Repetition can create unity within a work of art.
• Op Art is an art style in which an impression of movement is created on the picture surface by means of optical illusion, also known as Optical Art or Perceptual Abstraction.

DO:
• Students will identify repetition and variety of lines in a work of art.
• Students will use pattern to create a detailed optical illusion.
• Students will learn about and use complementary colors in a piece of artwork.

VOCABULARY:

Hexagon – A polygon with six edges and six vertices. A vertex (plural: vertices) is a corner or a point where two or more straight lines meet.

Illusion – A deceptive or misleading image or idea.

Op Art – An art style in which an impression of movement is created on the picture surface by means of optical illusion, also known as Optical Art or Perceptual Abstraction.

Optical Illusion – An image that deceives a person, leading to a misinterpretation of its meaning.

Parallel – Two or more straight lines or edges on the same plane that do not intersect. Parallel lines have the same direction.

Pattern – The repetition of shapes, lines or colors.

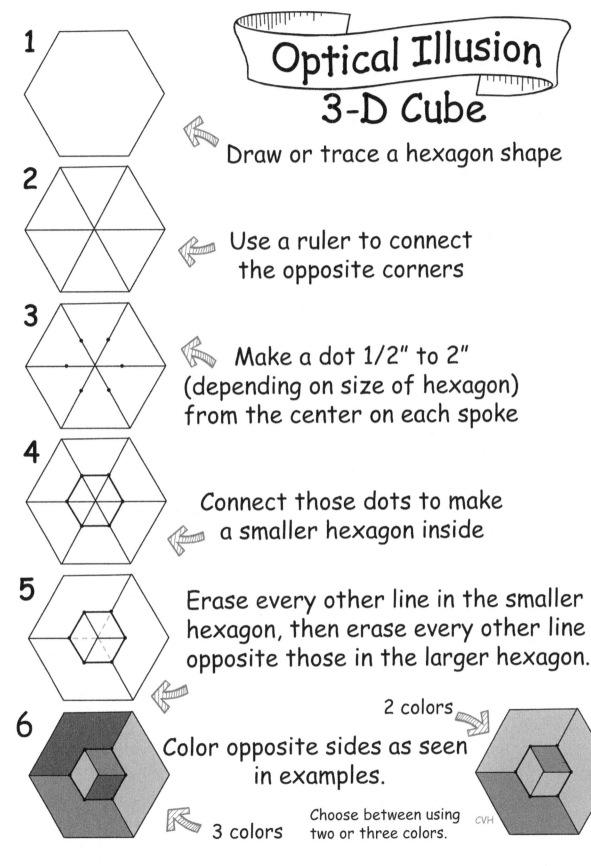

1 Draw or trace a hexagon shape

2 Use a ruler to connect the opposite corners

3 Make a dot 1/2" to 2" (depending on size of hexagon) from the center on each spoke

4 Connect those dots to make a smaller hexagon inside

5 Erase every other line in the smaller hexagon, then erase every other line opposite those in the larger hexagon.

6 Color opposite sides as seen in examples.

2 colors

3 colors

Choose between using two or three colors.

CVH

Optical Illusion
3-D Cube

OP ART HAND

KNOW:
Illusion, Op-Art, Parallel, Pattern

UNDERSTAND:
• Repetition can create unity within a work of art.
• Op Art is an art style in which an impression of movement is created on the picture surface by means of optical illusion, also known as Optical Art or Perceptual Abstraction.

DO:
• Students will identify repetition and variety of lines in a work of art.
• Students will use pattern to create a detailed optical illusion.
• Students will add color and pattern for interest.

VOCABULARY:
Illusion – A deceptive or misleading image or idea.

Op Art – An art style in which an impression of movement is created on the picture surface by means of optical illusion, also known as Optical Art or Perceptual Abstraction.

Parallel – Two or more straight lines or edges on the same plane that do not intersect. Parallel lines have the same direction.

Pattern – The repetition of shapes, lines or colors.

Op Art Hand

① Start by tracing your hand palm down.

end wrist with a curved line

add a straight line to both sides of wrist

TIP: To get the best hand shape, keep your pencil at a 90°angle.

② Draw another curved line above the one you just drew. Draw the straight lines as well. (Make sure the straight lines are parallel)

③ Repeat step 2 all the way up into the fingers. Curve each finger individually. The lines outside of the hand will stay straight.

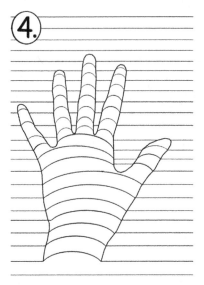

④ Once the hand curves are complete, add straight lines above and below until your paper is full.

⑤ Erase your original hand tracing. Be careful not to erase the curves and straight lines you just made.

⑥ Color! Make every other line an alternating color or create your own repetitive pattern to complete the illusion.

STRAIGHT LINE SPIRAL

KNOW:
Parabolic curves, Spiral

UNDERSTAND:
How to create a spiral using only straight lines.

DO:
The basic principle of this design is the creation of curved shapes from the intersection of straight lines. Students will follow the "Straight Line Spiral" worksheet to help them understand how to make a parabolic curve. Students will use inspiration and the tutorial provided to create their own unique Straight Line Spiral.

TIPS:
• Leave no more than one finger width at the base of each triangle drawn for the best results.
• Add details such as pattern, texture or shading to make it your own!

VOCABULARY:
Line – Any line that is clearly drawn and marks direction. Line is one of the seven Elements of Art; a moving dot with direction.

Parabolic Line Patterns – Repeated straight lines that eventually appear to create curves in art and architecture.

Spiral – A curve on a plane that winds around a fixed center point at a continuously increasing or decreasing distance from the point.

use a ruler!

Straight Line Spiral

This can be done with a square or a rectangle

1. Draw a straight line from the top left corner of the paper to the top right edge leaving space as shown.

leave a bit of space here

2. Next, draw a straight line from where the last line ended to the lower right edge as shown to form another long triangle.

here

to here

3. Next, draw a straight line from where that line ended to the bottom left corner.

here

to here

4. Finally, draw a straight line from where that line ended to the upper left edge. Repeat steps 1-4.

5. Keep going until there is no more space to draw lines.

6. This will create four rounded curves made from straight lines. The closer the lines, the rounder they appear.

STRAIGHT LINE HEART

KNOW:
Parabolic curves, Symmetry

UNDERSTAND:
How to create a heart using only straight lines.

DO:
The basic principle of this design is the creation of curved shapes from the intersection of straight lines. Students will follow the "Straight Line Heart" worksheet to help them understand how to make a parabolic curve. Students will use inspiration and the tutorial provided to create their own unique Straight Line Heart.

TIPS:
• Leave no more than one finger width at the base of each triangle drawn for the best results.
• Add details such as pattern, texture or shading to make it your own!

VOCABULARY:
Line – Any line that is clearly drawn and marks direction. Line is one of the seven Elements of Art; a moving dot with direction.

Parabolic Line Patterns – Repeated straight lines that eventually appear to create curves in art and architecture.

Symmetry - The parts of an image or object organized so that one side duplicates or mirrors the other.

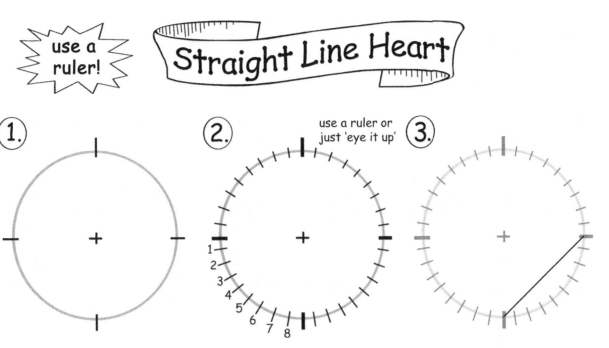

Straight Line Heart

use a ruler!

(1.)

(2.) use a ruler or just 'eye it up' **(3.)**

Start by lightly drawing a circle, find the center and make marks at 90 degree intervals as seen above.

TIP: Try and find a circle to trace

Make small marks at 10 degree intervals all the way around the circle. There should be eight marks between each line made in step 1.

Draw a line connecting two of the main marks as seen above. This will become part of the pointy base of the heart.

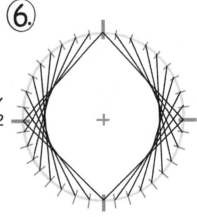

(4.)

Next, connect the mark to the right of mark "3" to the mark directly above mark "2" (shown with arrows). Continue to connect the marks this way.

(5.)

Stop when mark 2 is connected to mark 1 (indicated above by arrows).

(6.)

Do the same thing on the opposite side.

next >

Straight Line Heart continued . . .

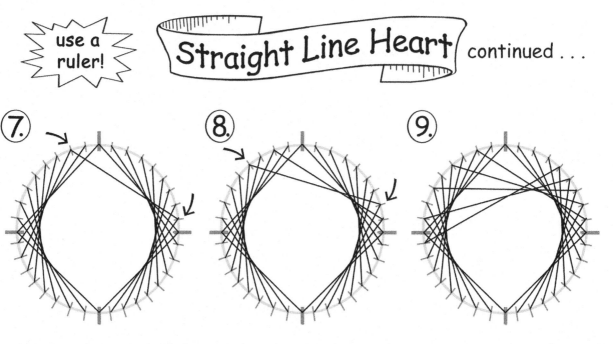

⑦. Count two lines to the left of the center, upper mark and start the next line. Connect it to the first line next to the 90 degree mark on the right side of the circle. (See arrows)

⑧. Count two more lines over from the left of the mark started in step 7. Connect it to the second line next to the 90 degree mark on the right side of the circle. (See arrows)

⑨. Keep connecting the marks by counting two marks for the starting point of the lines and two marks for the ending points.

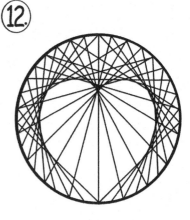

⑩. Continue until that side is complete. Pay close attention because this can get confusing!

⑪. Repeat on the opposite side.

⑫. Erase the guide marks and darken the circle when artwork is complete. Color if desired.

ANAMORPHIC WRITING

KNOW:
Anamorphic Art, Distortion

UNDERSTAND:
Text painted on roads as signage and directional arrows are designed anamorphically (stretched out) so that these signs are easily understood by the drivers who must view them obliquely.

DO:
View and discuss images of anamorphic art. Choose a word or phrase that has six or more letters that you will "draw" onto graph paper. Holding your paper vertically, use a ruler to create one letter per grid column, stretching your letters so they are just a few rows from the top and bottom of your paper. Continue writing each letter until the word is complete.

TIPS:
• Leave at least two spaces between each word and a half to one full column space between each letter so the words will be easier to read.
• Go over your letters in marker after you draw them in pencil so they stand out.
• Create one letter per column but use two columns for wider letters like "M" and "W".
• Share your work with others and see if they can read what you designed!

VOCABULARY:
Anamorphosis and Anamorphic Art – An image appears distorted because it is constructed on an elongated grid, rendering it unintelligible until it is viewed from a specific point of view or reflected in a curved mirror. "Anamorphosis" is a Greek word meaning transformation.

Distort – To change the way something looks; sometimes deforming or stretching an object or figure out of its normal shape to exaggerate its features to make it more interesting or meaningful.

Line – Any line that is clearly drawn and marks direction. Line is one of the seven Elements of Art; a moving dot with direction.

Oblique - Neither perpendicular nor parallel to a given line or surface; slanting; sloping.

Example of Distortion in Art: Hans Holbein (German, 1497/8-1543) created "The Ambassadors," an oil painting of two men posing with some objects. A human skull is painted in the lower third of the painting but appears distorted. The skull appears undistorted only when the painting is viewed at an angle.

Anamorphic Writing

1. Hold a piece of graph paper vertically. Choose a word to write that has at least six or more letters in it.

vertical

2. Using a ruler, create one letter per column.

stretch your letters so they are just a few rows from the top and a few rows from the bottom (letter D ›)

3. Skip one column space the start the next letter.

leave half to one full column space between letters so the word is easier to read later

skip 1 full or 1/2 column between letters

4. Continue until the word is complete. Skip two columns to start a new word.

make sure your letters start and end at the same row line

5. Tilt your paper at an extreme angle so your words are easier to read.

TIPS:

Go over your letters with a bright colored marker so they stand out

Always use a ruler

Create one letter per column but use two columns for wider letters like "M" or "W"

Share your work with your friends and test them to see if they can read your anamorphic writing!

149

IMPOSSIBLE OBJECTS

An **impossible object** is a type of optical illusion.

Optical illusions are images that are often described as visual images that differ from reality; the information gathered by the eye is processed by the brain and creates a perception that does not match the true image. As we take information in through our eyes, our brain tries to interpret what we see to make sense; however, an optical illusion tricks us into seeing things that cannot exist in the real world. These impossible constructions violate the laws of geometry.

When viewing an **impossible object**, the initial impression of a 3D object is offered but the impossibility usually becomes apparent after viewing the figure for a few seconds.

Our eyes want to interpret these drawings as three-dimensional objects but they are not based in reality upon closer inspection. The lines connect in unrealistic ways that are unsettling. Looking at different parts of the object makes one reassess the 3D nature of the object, which confuses the mind.

Although possible to represent in two dimensions, it is not geometrically possible for these objects to exist in the physical world. Some 3D constructions of impossible objects have been created that offer the idea of an impossible object when viewed from a very specific point. This cannot be considered a 3D representation of an impossible object in the true sense of construction because the illusion cannot be maintained when the object is rotated or the viewpoint is changed.

There are hundreds of impossible objects that can be created through drawing and there is just a fraction of that amount on the next few pages.

What impossible objects can you create?

THE IMPOSSIBLE TRIANGLE

KNOW:
Equilateral triangle, Parallel lines, Optical illusion

UNDERSTAND:
• Our brain puts information together in a way that makes sense and allows us to see optical illusions in different ways.
• How to create the illusion of an Impossible Triangle where the beams of the triangle simultaneously appear to recede and come toward you.

DO:
• Students will view optical illusions and discuss how the brain can be deceived by puzzling visual challenges.
• View and discuss examples of "Impossible" objects in art.
• Using the tips and guidelines provided, students will test and enhance the power of their observation and critical thinking skills by creating their version of the Impossible Triangle using measurements and shading.

TIP: Before drawing dark, permanent lines with a ruler, lightly sketch guidelines to indicate the general area of the lines in each step. It is very difficult to draw these lines perfectly without measurements.

VOCABULARY:
Gradual – A smooth transition from dark to light values; little by little.

Equilateral Triangle - A triangle in which all three sides are equal.

Parallel Lines - Two lines on a plane that never meet.

Penrose Triangle - Also known as the "Penrose Tribar" or "Impossible Triangle", this impossible object was first created by the Swedish artist Oscar Reutersvärd in 1934 who drew his version of a triangle as a set of cubes in parallel projection. It is featured prominently in the works of artist M. C. Escher, whose earlier depictions of impossible objects partly inspired it. His version was painted as three bars connected with right angles.

Optical Illusion – An image that deceives a person, leading to a misinterpretation of its meaning.

More information: In 1961, artist M.C. Escher created the lithograph "Waterfall" based on the principles of the Impossible Triangle.

Also known as the "Penrose Triangle"

The Impossible Triangle

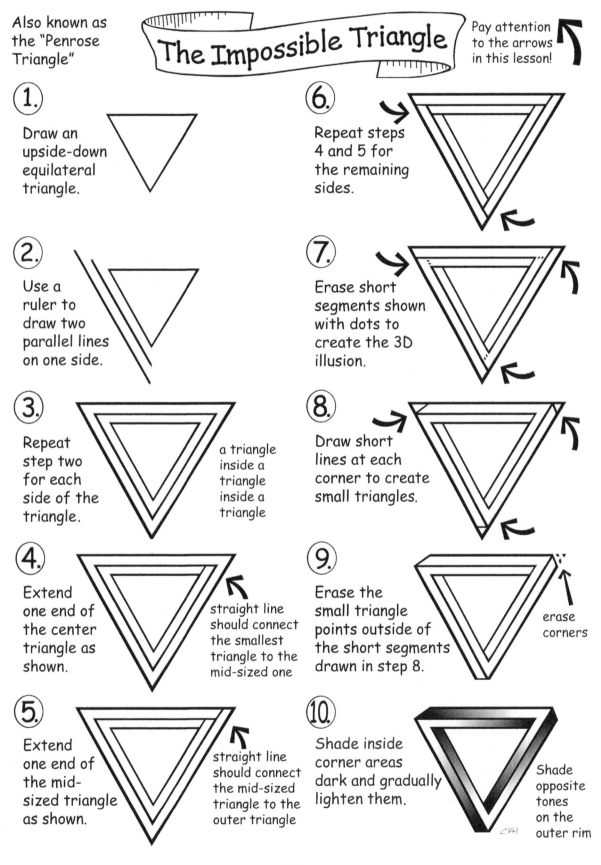

Pay attention to the arrows in this lesson!

1. Draw an upside-down equilateral triangle.

2. Use a ruler to draw two parallel lines on one side.

3. Repeat step two for each side of the triangle.

a triangle inside a triangle inside a triangle

4. Extend one end of the center triangle as shown.

straight line should connect the smallest triangle to the mid-sized one

5. Extend one end of the mid-sized triangle as shown.

straight line should connect the mid-sized triangle to the outer triangle

6. Repeat steps 4 and 5 for the remaining sides.

7. Erase short segments shown with dots to create the 3D illusion.

8. Draw short lines at each corner to create small triangles.

9. Erase the small triangle points outside of the short segments drawn in step 8.

erase corners

10. Shade inside corner areas dark and gradually lighten them.

Shade opposite tones on the outer rim

The Impossible Square

Pay attention to the arrows in this lesson!

1. Draw a square.

2. Use a ruler to draw two parallel lines on one side.

3. Repeat step 2 for each side of the square.

a square inside a square inside a square

4. Extend one end of the center square.

a straight line connects smallest square to the mid-sized one

5. Extend one end of the mid-sized square as shown.

6. Repeat steps 4 and 5 for the remaining sides.

7. Erase short segments shown with dots to create the 3D illusion.

8. Draw short lines at each corner to make small triangles.

9. Erase the small triangle points outside of the short segments drawn above.

erase corners

10. Shade the inside corner areas dark & gradually lighten them.

Shade each touching section the opposite of one another

154

THE IMPOSSIBLE HEART

KNOW:
Horizontal, Parallel lines, Optical Illusion

UNDERSTAND:
• Our brain puts information together in a way that makes sense and allows us to see optical illusions in different ways.
• The importance of using guidelines for accuracy when drawing.
• How to create the illusion of an Impossible Heart where the beams and curves of the heart simultaneously appear to recede and come toward you.

DO:
• Students will view optical illusions and discuss how the brain can be deceived by puzzling visual challenges.
• View and discuss examples of "Impossible" objects in art.
• Students will test and enhance the power of their observation and critical thinking skills by creating their version of the Impossible Heart using measurements and shading.

VOCABULARY:
Curve – A continuously bending line, without angles.

Gradual – A smooth transition from dark to light values; little by little.

Guide Lines – A lightly marked line used as a guide when composing a drawing.

Horizontal Lines – Straight and flat across, parallel to the horizon. The opposite is vertical.

Optical Illusion – An image that deceives a person, leading to a misinterpretation of its meaning.

Parallel Lines - Two lines on a plane that never meet.

Interesting Fact: Many people think that the Impossible Triangle is actually impossible to construct, however, it was proved that all impossible figures are possible. A three-dimensional object that looks impossible from a single point of view can be created. It would look ordinary from all other points of view.

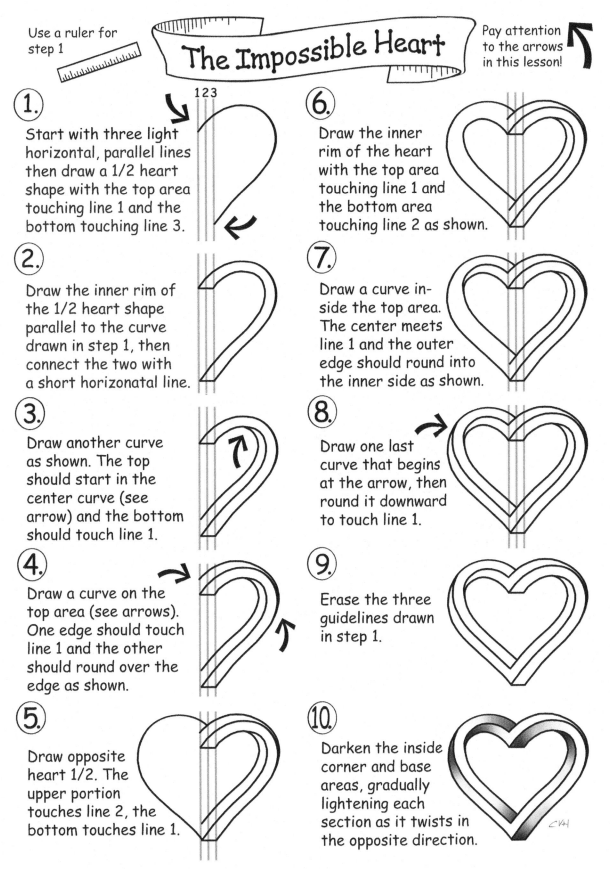

Use a ruler for step 1

The Impossible Heart

Pay attention to the arrows in this lesson!

1. Start with three light horizontal, parallel lines then draw a 1/2 heart shape with the top area touching line 1 and the bottom touching line 3.

2. Draw the inner rim of the 1/2 heart shape parallel to the curve drawn in step 1, then connect the two with a short horizonatal line.

3. Draw another curve as shown. The top should start in the center curve (see arrow) and the bottom should touch line 1.

4. Draw a curve on the top area (see arrows). One edge should touch line 1 and the other should round over the edge as shown.

5. Draw opposite heart 1/2. The upper portion touches line 2, the bottom touches line 1.

6. Draw the inner rim of the heart with the top area touching line 1 and the bottom area touching line 2 as shown.

7. Draw a curve inside the top area. The center meets line 1 and the outer edge should round into the inner side as shown.

8. Draw one last curve that begins at the arrow, then round it downward to touch line 1.

9. Erase the three guidelines drawn in step 1.

10. Darken the inside corner and base areas, gradually lightening each section as it twists in the opposite direction.

157

THE IMPOSSIBLE HEXAGON

KNOW:
Equilateral Triangle, Hexagon, Parallel lines, Optical illusion

UNDERSTAND:
• Our brain puts information together in a way that makes sense and allows us to see optical illusions in different ways.
• How to create the illusion of an Impossible Hexagon where the angles simultaneously appear to recede and come toward you.

DO:
• Students will view optical illusions and discuss how the brain can be deceived by puzzling visual challenges.
• View and discuss examples of "Impossible" objects in art.
• Using the tips and guidelines provided, students will test and enhance the power of their observation and critical thinking skills by creating their version of the Impossible Hexagon using measurements and shading.

VOCABULARY:
Gradual – A smooth transition from dark to light values; little by little.

Hexagon - A polygon having six angles and six sides.

Parallel Lines - Two lines on a plane that never meet.

Optical Illusion – An image that deceives a person, leading to a misinterpretation of its meaning.

The Impossible Hexagon

1. Draw a light cross shape as a guide. Draw a hexagon.

← triangle

upside down trapezoid

2. Use a ruler to draw two parallel lines on one side.

3. Repeat step 2 for each side. Erase the cross.

hexagon inside a hexagon inside a hexagon

4. Extend one end of the center hexagon.

5. Extend one end of the mid-sized hexagon as shown.

6. Repeat steps 4 and 5 for the remaining sides.

7. Erase short segments shown with dots to create the 3D illusion.

8. Draw short lines at each corner to make small triangles.

9. Erase the small triangle points outside of the short segments drawn above.

erase corners

10. Shade the inside corner areas dark & gradually lighten them.

THE IMPOSSIBLE STAR OF DAVID

KNOW:
Equilateral Triangle, Hexagon, Parallel lines, Optical illusion, Star of David

UNDERSTAND:
• Our brain puts information together in a way that makes sense and allows us to see optical illusions in different ways.
• Because of its geometric symmetry, the hexagram has been a popular symbol in many cultures from the earliest times.
• How to create the illusion of an Impossible Star of David where the beams of the hexagon simultaneously appear to recede and come toward you at the same time.

DO:
• Students will view optical illusions and discuss how the brain can be deceived by puzzling visual challenges.
• View and discuss examples of "Impossible" objects in art.
• Using the tips and guidelines provided, students will test and enhance the power of their observation and critical thinking skills by creating their version of the Impossible Star of David using measurements and shading.

VOCABULARY:
Gradual – A smooth transition from dark to light values; little by little.

Equilateral Triangle - A triangle in which all three sides are equal.

Hexagon - A polygon having six angles and six sides.

Parallel Lines - Two lines on a plane that never meet.

Optical Illusion – An image that deceives a person, leading to a misinterpretation of its meaning.

Star of David – Also known in Hebrew as the **Shield of David** or **Magen David** is a generally recognized symbol of modern Jewish identity in the shape of a hexagram, the compound of two equilateral triangles. The Star of David is not a uniquely a Jewish symbol.

use a ruler!

Impossible Star of David

1. Draw a triangle, inside a triangle, inside a triangle.

2. Extend some of the lines so they touch the triangle next to it.

3. Draw short lines at each corner to make small triangles.

4. Draw a large, upside down triangle as shown.

5. Draw a triangle inside the triangle drawn in step 4.

Erase the triangle points outside the short segments drawn in step 3.

6. Draw another triangle inside that triangle. Draw short lines at each corner.

7. Erase the triangle points outside the short segments drawn in step 6.

8. Erase areas indicated by the dashed lines as shown. Look carefully!

9. Add lines where indicated so that they are connected as shown.

10. Shade the inside corner areas dark & gradually lighten the plane until it's white.

Shade each touching section the opposite of one another

THE ENDLESS STAIRCASE
Also known as **"The Impossible Staircase"** or **"The Penrose Staircase"**

KNOW:
Perspective Distortion

UNDERSTAND:
• Our brain puts information together in a way that makes sense and allows us to see optical illusions in different ways.
• How to create the illusion of an Impossible Staircase where the highest or lowest step cannot be determined.

DO:
• Students will view optical illusions and discuss how the brain can be deceived by puzzling visual challenges.
• View and discuss examples of "The Impossible Staircase," following the staircase around and trying to determine the lowest or highest step. What happens when the eye follows the stairs in a clockwise direction? In a counter-clockwise direction?
• Using the tips and guidelines provided, students will test and enhance the power of their observation and critical thinking skills by creating their own version of the Endless Staircase using measurements and shading.

VOCABULARY:
Gradual – A smooth transition from dark to light values; little by little.

Parallel Lines - Two lines on a plane that never meet.

Perspective Distortion – An image that appears normal because different regions of the image are focused upon. Each of those regions makes sense alone, but viewed together they create an impossible situation.

Optical Illusion – An image that deceives a person, leading to a misinterpretation of its meaning.

More information: A figure by the mathematician L.S. Penrose, this was idea was used as the basis for M.C. Eschers artwork: "Ascending and Descending".

1.
2. ↓
basic cube
3.
4. ↓

Endless Staircase

1. Start with a basic cube that is elongated vertically.

Extend base lines at angle as shown

2. Add another elongated cube to the right of the first. This one is slightly taller.

shorter   taller

Use existing base line for the bottom of cube

3. Add a third elongated cube to the right of the second. This should be slightly taller than the second.

taller →
shorter →

4. Fill the entire left line with cubes.

Each cube gets lower

Start here (at #1) then keep adding cubes to the left

6 5 4 3 2 1

5. Add two more cubes that ascend from the cube drawn in step 3.

Leave off this line →

6. Working from left to right, add descending cubes at the back.

1 2 3 4

7. Add the last cube. It should overlap a tiny bit as shown.

8. Erase the part of the cube "underneath" as shown.

Erase lines "inside" the staircase

9. Shade the inside left wall and outside right wall dark as shown.

Chapter 5

Cool Stuff

CHAIN LINK HEART LOCK

KNOW:
Overlapping, Pattern, Repetition

UNDERSTAND:
• The elements of a pattern repeat in a predictable manner.
• How to create the appearance of interlocking forms by using overlapping techniques and shading.

DO:
• Create a realistic chain of interlocking links using the tips and tricks provided.
• Loop a unique shape (such as the heart shown) through the links as a "lock" fixture.
• Shade.
• Erase some areas on each link to create a metallic "shine" effect.

VOCABULARY:
Overlapping – When one thing lies over and partly covers something else.

Pattern – The repetition of shapes, lines or colors.

Repetition – A way of combining elements of art so that the same elements are used over and over again.

Chain Heart Lock

Draw lightly . . . there will be a bit of erasing

1. Start with 2 ovals.

↑ overlap

2. Add triangle below.

Triangle goes through base of circles

Edges touch

3. Erase lines inside.

4. Draw 1/2 oval at top of heart as shown below.

5. Add two chain links at a slight angle.

overlap   overlap

These look a bit like rounded rectangles

6. Draw two ovals on both sides as shown.

An oval inside an oval

Erase dotted line

7. Add two more links. Angle them upward.

Erase dotted areas inside both links

8. Draw another oval

on each side as shown.

9. Add rounded rectangles at each end.

Keep adding links until the space is filled.

10. Curve links upward as you draw them

11. Erase some areas near the "front" of each link for highlights

Shade below the rounded retangles so they appear "on top" of the ovals

Shade and add a keyhole.

HOURGLASS

KNOW:
Geometric shapes, Highlight, Texture, Transparent, Value

UNDERSTAND:
• Shading using value will achieve a more realistic rendering.
• A transparent object allows us to see through a form.
• The difference between shape and form.
• How to arrange elements in an artwork so that they appear symmetrical or equally balanced.
• How to create an effective design using simple shapes.
• How to create the appearance of texture.

DO:
• Follow the steps provided to create an original Hourglass design that starts with two simple circles connected then shaded to create a complex form.
• Use learned 3D techniques which concentrate on overlapping and shading to convey the illusion of depth.
• Create the illusion of transparency showing sand texture through the glass.

VOCABULARY:
Balance - A principle of design, balance refers to the way the elements of art are arranged to create a feeling of stability in a work; a pleasing or harmonious arrangement or proportion of parts or areas in a design or composition.

Curve – A line or edge that deviates from straightness in a smooth, continuous way or, something that has the shape of a curve, such as an arc.

Highlight - The area on any surface which reflects the most light; to direct attention to or emphasize an area of a drawing through use of value.

Texture - The way something looks like it might feel like in an artwork. Simulated textures are suggested by an artist with different brushstrokes, pencil lines, etc.

Transparent - Allowing light to pass through so that objects can be clearly seen on the other side; the opposite of opaque.

Texture – The technique an artist uses to make an object look like it feels a certain way.

Value - An element of art that refers to the lightness or darkness of a color.

Hourglass

① Start with 2 circles.

leave space in between

② Add 2 curved lines.

curve

almost touches circle

③ Add four more lines.

overlaps a bit of circle

lower

same at bottom

④ Round edges as shown.

close the ends

erase area indicated with dots

⑤ Connect with curves.

curve inward

⑥ Connect top & base.

erase dotted areas

⑦

Add detail to lines.

erase dotted areas

⑧

add "sand" passing from top to bottom

add lines to indicate transparency

⑨

Shade.

erase some spots for "highlights"

add dots for sand texture

BASEBALL CAP

KNOW:
• Simple shapes combined together can create more complex objects
• How to create a sense of depth in an artwork

UNDERSTAND:
Differences in the size of object parts can help to achieve the illusion of depth.

DO:
Create an original artwork of your version of a baseball cap that shows depth following the steps provided. Don't trace. Shade.

VOCABULARY:
Oval – An egg-like, two-dimensional shape that looks like a circle but has been stretched to make it longer. The two ends of an oval may or may not be the same size and shape.

Perspective – The technique used to create the illusion of 3D onto a 2D surface. Perspective helps to create a sense of depth or receding space.

Trapezoid - A quadrilateral plane figure having two parallel and two nonparallel sides. (A quadrilateral is a plane figure having four sides and four angles.)

Baseball Cap

Curved Brim

1. 1/2 oval — trapezoid

Start with a trapezoid with a 1/2 oval on top.

2. Erase dotted areas

Add a slightly rounded line at base.

3. Angle a square shape for the brim.

4. add grommets — Erase dotted areas

Round the brim and add curved lines on the cap as shown.

5. Draw curved lines on brim for stitch detail.

6. Shade as desired.

Flat Brim

1. Start with a rectangle and a 1/2 oval on top. Erase dotted.

2. Add angled shape. Erase dotted area at base

Round the base of the rectangle slightly as shown.

3. Round the brim. Add grommets and stitching.

4. Erase dotted areas.

5. Add logo and shade.

Dexter

ART

173

BOBBLEHEAD RAGDOLL

KNOW:
You can make original cartoon-style creatures by using geometric shapes.

UNDERSTAND:
• To make a work original, that work must have elements that are not copied or traced.
• Expressive qualities in your drawing add a feeling, mood or idea to your character.

DO:
Practice creating an original, ragdoll style character using the geometric guidelines provided. Draw lightly so guidelines can be erased if needed. Add or change certain elements as necessary to make it unique. Try to create a character NOT seen on the handout. Use your imagination and add a lot of "extras".

NOTE: The steps outlined in this tutorial are just a few examples of the thousands of ideas you could choose to create an original character. Use these guidelines or choose whatever shapes and features work for your original character.

VOCABULARY:
Cartoon – A simple drawing created to get people thinking, angry, laughing, or otherwise amused. A cartoon usually has simple lines, uses basic colors, and tells a story in one or a series of pictures called frames or panels.

Expressive Qualities - The feelings, moods and ideas communicated to the viewer through a work of art.

Original – Any work considered to be an authentic example of the works of an artist, rather than a reproduction, imitation or a copy.

Bobblehead Ragdoll

1. Start with a body made from simple shapes . . .

2. Next, choose an expressive set of eyes - draw them small and set them far apart.

3. Then, choose an expressive mouth and nose to work with your eyes.

4. Finally, add as many details as you need to build a unique, interesting character.

try different combinations of features and outfits

add details and patterns

don't forget shoes and hair accessories

CVH

HUMAN HEART

KNOW:
The human heart is a muscle that sends blood around your body, giving it the oxygen it needs. The average human heart pumps about 70 milliliters of blood with every beat. That's about five liters every minute or about 7,200 liters every day.

UNDERSTAND:
The major parts of the human heart

DO:
Students will draw their own version of the human heart and label the major parts.

NOTE:
There are many different angles and views of the human heart. This is just one of them!

VOCABULARY:
Heart – A muscular organ about the size of a closed fist that lies to the left of the chest and functions as the body's circulatory pump.

Inferior vena cava – Also known as the posterior vena cava, is the large vein that carries deoxygenated blood from the lower half of the body into the right atrium of the heart.

Left atrium – One of four chambers in the heart that receives oxygenated blood from the pulmonary veins, and pumps it into the left ventricle via the mitral valve.

Pulmonary artery – Carries deoxygenated blood from the heart to the lungs.

Pulmonary veins - Large blood vessels that receive oxygenated blood from the lungs and drain into the left atrium of the heart. There are four pulmonary veins, two from each lung.

Right atrium - One of four chambers in the heart. It receives deoxygenated blood and pumps it into the right ventricle through the tricuspid valve.

Right/Left ventricle – One of two large chambers that collect and expel blood received from an atrium towards the peripheral beds within the body and lungs.

Superior vena cava – Vein that carries deoxygenated blood from the upper half of the body to the heart's right atrium.

Human Heart

1. Lightly draw a circle. Add a rounded tip at the side bottom. This will be the main heart.

extend & round the base

2. Add a similar shape to the upper left as shown. Erase dotted line.

3. Erase area inside the shape drawn in step 2. Add a smaller 1/2 oval on the right.

left atrium

right atrium

4. Add a curved shape that overlaps as shown. This will be the pulmonary artery.

Add two small curves

5. Add a "Y" shaped tube extending from the right atrium. This will be the Superior vena cava.

Erase dotted areas inside as shown

6. Add arch connecting Superior vena cava to pulmonary artery.

aorta

7. Draw three tubes at the top curve of the aorta. Erase dotted.

8. Add more tubes as shown. Erase dotted.

9. Add veins. Label parts if desired.

superior vena cava

right atrium

right ventricle

inferior vena cava

aorta

pulmonary artery

left atrium

pulmonary veins

left ventricle

PALM OF THE HAND

KNOW:
Creating a likeness from observation

UNDERSTAND:
• Shading using value scale tones will achieve a more realistic rendering.

• Drawn objects that appear close to us are large and usually close to the bottom of the page. Objects that appear farther from us in a drawing are usually small and higher on the page.

DO:
• Practice drawing your hand using observation and the proposed techniques.

• Make the darkest values between the fingers and knuckle creases. This will indicate texture of the skin. Erase some spots on the finger pads and between the creases to create a natural highlight effect.

VOCABULARY:
Highlight - The area on any surface which reflects the most light; to direct attention to or emphasize an area of a drawing through use of value.

Perspective – The technique used to create the illusion of 3D onto a 2D surface. Perspective helps to create a sense of depth or receding space.

Texture - The way something looks like it might feel like in an artwork. Simulated textures are suggested by an artist with different brushstrokes, pencil lines, etc.

Palm of the Hand

1. Start with a long rectangle. Trim as seen below.

erase dotted line

angle

2. Add two ovals at left.

small angled oval at top, larger on bottom

overlap

3. Draw two more lean ovals for the thumb.

angle

4. Add a curve for fingers and three ovals for the pinky.

connect

overlapping ovals indicate finger joints

5. Draw three more overlapping ovals for ring finger.

extends farther than the pinky

6. Draw three more ovals for the middle finger.

longer than ring finger

7. erase dotted

Draw three more ovals for the pointer finger.

shorter than middle finger

8. Add hand crease details.

9. Shade.

CVH

179

KOI FISH

KNOW:
- Simple shapes combined together can create more complex objects
- Overlapping
- Adding extra elements to a drawing can create interest and tell a story
- Scalloped Texture, Layer

UNDERSTAND:
- Overlapping simple shapes can be the first step to creating complex forms.
- Overlapping and layering items help to create a sense of depth and realism.

DO:
Create an original artwork of a koi fish following the steps provided. Use shading and scalloped texture for realism. Add "extras" including a background or Asian symbols for interest.

VOCABULARY:

Detail – A part of a whole. A distinctive feature of an object or scene which can be seen most clearly close up.

Layer – Something placed over another surface (layering the scales).

Overlap - When one thing lies over, partly covering something else. Depicting this is one of the most important means of conveying an illusion of depth.

Scallop – One of a series of similar curves that form a decorative edge on something.

Texture - The way something looks like it might feel like in an artwork. Simulated textures are suggested by an artist with different brushstrokes, pencil lines, etc.

Add a peaceful symbol to your work

水

Japan symbol for water

Draw a Koi

光明

Japan symbol for glory, hope, bright future

1. Start with a circle. Draw a curved line dividing the shape.

like this

2. Erase the dotted area. Add a lip, eye and fin.

rounded lip

3. Add a point shape here.

Curve a line down the back for fins.

Add a small curve here.

4. Add two curved lines at tail.

Draw curved head

Add fin

Erase

5. close tail with scalloped "V"

Add detail to fin line on back

6. **TIPS**

start with a 1/2 circle

add another touching it

add another in between

Start adding scales.

7. Fill the body with scales.

8. Add fin detail.

Add whiskers

9. Add design in background.

Shade. 光明

Add symbols

181

TEDDY BEAR

KNOW:
• Simple shapes combined together can create more complex objects
• Layering, Overlapping
• Adding extra elements to a drawing can create interest and tell a story
• Texture

UNDERSTAND:
• Overlapping simple shapes can be the first step to creating complex forms.
• Overlapping and layering items help to create a sense of depth and realism.
• The techniques an artist uses to show how something might feel or what it is made of in an artwork.

DO:
Follow the steps provided and create your own version of a teddy bear. Begin with layering simple geometric shapes and connecting them to create a more complex, organic forms. Add "Extras" like fur and stitching. Shade.

VOCABULARY:
Layering – To place something over another surface or object.

Overlap - When one thing lies over, partly covering something else. Depicting this is one of the most important means of conveying an illusion of depth.

Texture - The way something looks like it might feel like in an artwork. Simulated textures are suggested by an artist with different brushstrokes, pencil lines, etc.

Teddy Bear

1. Start with three circles; two at the top and one near the bottom.

small

large

push this one over to the right a bit

2. Add ovals for ears.

Erase dotted areas

3. Lightly draw two ovals for the arm.

Erase dotted areas

4. Add second arm on right as shown.

connect shoulder

connect head to belly

Erase dotted areas

slight overlap

5. Add two ovals for feet.

space here

6. Connect feet to body.

add ear & nose details

7. Add eyes and mouth.

Erase dotted areas

Add belly button and belly wrinkles

8. Add paw detail on feet.

9. Shade and add texture.

Add "fuzzy" edges

THE "T" TRAIN

KNOW:
- Balance
- Elements of Design
- Highlight, Value
- Symmetry
- Simple shapes combined together can create more complex objects

UNDERSTAND:
- How to create a sense of depth in an artwork.
- Overlapping and differences in the size of objects in a scene help to achieve the illusion of depth.
- Drawn objects that appear close to us are large and usually close to the bottom of the page. Objects that appear farther from us in a drawing are usually small and higher on the page.
- Overlapping simple shapes can be the first step to creating complex forms.

DO:
Follow the steps provided to create a subway train that indicates perspective.

VOCABULARY:

Elements of Art or **Elements of Design** - The basic components used by the artist when producing works of art. Those elements are color, value, line, shape, form, texture, and space. The elements of art are among the literal qualities found in any artwork.

Perspective – The technique used to create the illusion of 3D onto a 2D surface. Perspective helps to create a sense of depth or receding space.

The "T" train

1. Start with a square.

2. Trim corners
Add curve at base.
(erase dotted)

3. Add a doorway
Add another curve at base.

4. Add headlights.

5. Add windows.

6. Round inner door.

7. Add window in door
Rectangle above door
Hook at front.

two circles

8. Add two small rectangles and line by door base.

9. Add "T" logo
Extend train so it to recedes.

10. Add windows.

11. Add receding track.

TYRANNOSAURUS REX

KNOW:
- Simple shapes combined together can create more complex objects
- Overlapping
- Adding extra elements to a drawing can create interest and tell a story
- Texture

UNDERSTAND:
- Overlapping simple shapes can be the first step to creating complex forms.
- Overlapping and layering items help to create a sense of depth and realism.

DO:
Create an original artwork of a Tyrannosaurus Rex following the steps provided. Use shading and texture for realism. Wrinkles indicate folds in the skin. Draw a background behind your dinosaur to create a scene.

VOCABULARY:
Detail – A part of a whole. A distinctive feature of an object or scene which can be seen most clearly close up.

Layer – Something placed over another surface.

Overlap - When one thing lies over, partly covering something else. Depicting this is one of the most important means of conveying an illusion of depth.

Perspective – The technique used to create the illusion of 3D onto a 2D surface. Perspective helps to create a sense of depth or receding space.

Texture - The way something looks like it might feel like in an artwork. Simulated textures are suggested by an artist with different brushstrokes, pencil lines, etc.

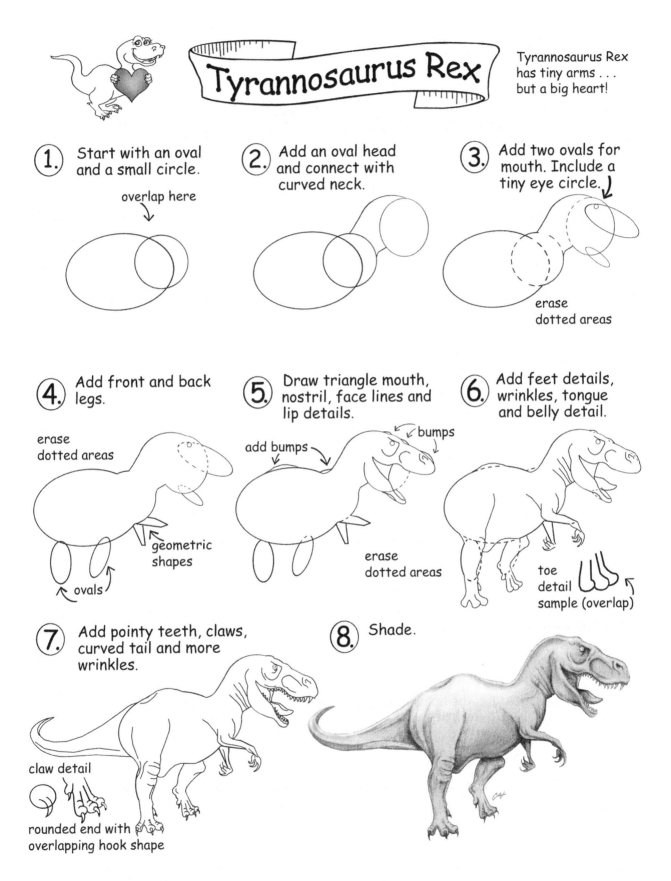

Tyrannosaurus Rex

Tyrannosaurus Rex has tiny arms . . . but a big heart!

1. Start with an oval and a small circle.

overlap here

2. Add an oval head and connect with curved neck.

3. Add two ovals for mouth. Include a tiny eye circle.

erase dotted areas

4. Add front and back legs.

erase dotted areas

geometric shapes

ovals

5. Draw triangle mouth, nostril, face lines and lip details.

add bumps

bumps

erase dotted areas

6. Add feet details, wrinkles, tongue and belly detail.

toe detail sample (overlap)

7. Add pointy teeth, claws, curved tail and more wrinkles.

claw detail

rounded end with overlapping hook shape

8. Shade.

SIMPLE SKELETON

KNOW:
• Simple shapes combined together can create more complex objects
• Layering, Overlapping
• Simple steps to create a realistic human skeleton
• Major bones of the body

UNDERSTAND:
• Overlapping simple shapes can be the first step to creating complex forms.
• The basics of proportion to create a human skull.
• Features of the human head can be measured/created on a grid.

DO:
Follow the steps provided and create your own version of a human skeleton. Begin with layering simple geometric shapes and connect them to create a more complex form.

VOCABULARY:
Femur - Thigh bone.

Fibula - Calf bone is a leg bone located on the lateral side of the tibia.

Humerus - Bone of the upper arm.

Layering – To place something over another surface or object.

Overlap - When one thing lies over, partly covering something else. Depicting this is one of the most important means of conveying an illusion of depth.

Pelvis - Ring-like structure of bones at the lower end of the trunk.

Radius - The shorter of the two long bones of the forearm.

Skull - Bony structure, the head in the skeleton, which supports the structures of the face and forms a cavity for the brain.

Spine - Vertebral column, also known as the backbone, is a bony structure found in vertebrates. It is formed from individual bones called vertebrae.

Tibia - The larger and stronger of the two bones in the leg below the knee in vertebrates.

Ulna - The longer of the two bones of the forearm, the other being the radius.

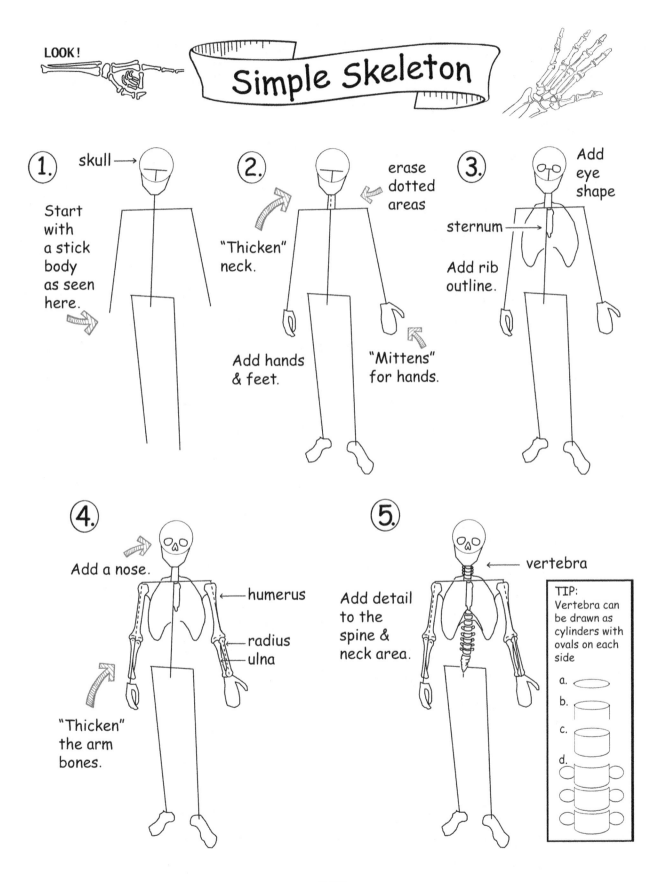

LOOK!

Simple Skeleton

1. skull → Start with a stick body as seen here.

2. "Thicken" neck. erase dotted areas. Add hands & feet. "Mittens" for hands.

3. Add eye shape. sternum → Add rib outline.

4. Add a nose. humerus radius ulna "Thicken" the arm bones.

5. Add detail to the spine & neck area. vertebra

TIP: Vertebra can be drawn as cylinders with ovals on each side

a.
b.
c.
d.

The adult human body is seven heads high

Simple Skeleton
continued

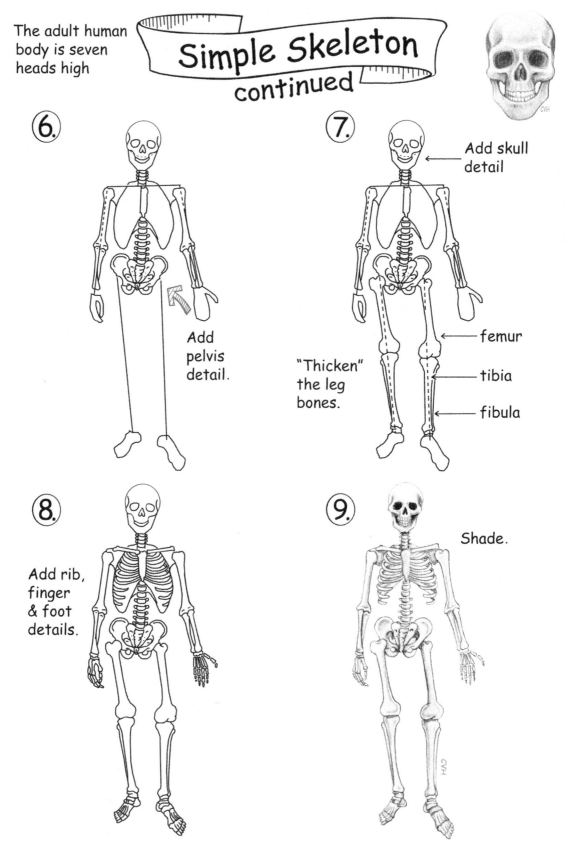

6. Add pelvis detail.

7. Add skull detail

"Thicken" the leg bones.

femur

tibia

fibula

8. Add rib, finger & foot details.

9. Shade.

CVH

DACHSHUND DOGGIE

KNOW:
Balance, Curve, Geometric shapes, Highlight

UNDERSTAND:
• Shading using value will achieve a more realistic rendering.
• The difference between shape and form.
• How to arrange elements in an artwork so that they appear symmetrical or equally balanced.
• How to create an effective design using simple shapes.
• Simple shapes combined together can create more complex objects.

DO:
• Practice breaking down complex objects into simple shapes by looking around the room at items and visually simplifying them.

• Follow the steps provided and create your own version of a dachshund dog. Begin by drawing simple geometric shapes and connecting them to create a more complex, organic shape that resembles the breed. Add "Extras" like wrinkles and texture. Shade to indicate form. Erase areas for highlights.

EXTRA CREDIT:
Follow the steps to draw a dog but place the body shape circles far apart to create a super-long pup! Hold your paper horizontally (or diagonally) for maximum length.

VOCABULARY:
Balance - A principle of design, balance refers to the way the elements of art are arranged to create a feeling of stability in a work; a pleasing or harmonious arrangement or proportion of parts or areas in a design or composition.

Combine – Two or more objects put together.

Curve – A line or edge that deviates from straightness in a smooth, continuous way or, something that has the shape of a curve, such as an arc.

Geometric Shape - A non-organic shape that utilizes rectilinear or simple curvilinear motifs or outlines in design.

Highlight - The area on any surface which reflects the most light; to direct attention to or emphasize an area of a drawing through use of value.

Texture - The way something looks like it might feel like in an artwork. Simulated textures are suggested by an artist with different brushstrokes, pencil lines, etc.

Dachshund Doggie

1. Start with two circles. The circle on the left should be larger.

distance between circles will determine how long dog will be

2. Add another small circle for the head. Connect the body.

3. Connect the head with curved lines. Erase dotted portions of the body circles as shown.

add 1/2 oval for muzzle

4. Add ovals for top of legs and paws. Add an angled ear.

erase circle parts in head not needed

5. Connect the legs. Add a tail and an eye.

bump

curve

bend

slight bump

6. Erase dotted areas as shown. Add a second set of legs "behind" the first set.

7. Add a nose, erase dotted area.

8. Add wrinkles in body, paw detail and mouth.

detail

9. Shade.

Try and make a super-long doggie!

HOT DOG

DEXTER THE CAT

KNOW:
Combine, Overlap, Proportion, Tubular

UNDERSTAND:
• Shading using value will achieve a more realistic rendering.
• The difference between shape and form.
• How to create an effective likeness of an oriental shorthair breed cat using simple shapes.
• Simple shapes combined together can create more complex objects.

DO:
• Practice breaking down complex objects into simple shapes by looking around the room at items and visually simplifying them.

• Follow the steps provided and create your own version of Dexter (or your own favorite kitty-cat). Begin by drawing simple geometric shapes and connecting them to create a more complex, organic shape that resembles the breed. Add "Extras" like fur texture, whiskers, collar, etc. Shade to indicate form or pattern. Erase areas for highlights.

VOCABULARY:
Combine – Two or more objects put together.

Overlap - When one thing lies over, partly covering something else. Depicting this is one of the most important means of conveying an illusion of depth.

Proportion - The proportion relationship of one part to another in an object or the whole object with respect to size, quantity, degree or number.

Tubular – Having a cylindrical body in the form or shape of a tube.

Dexter is an oriental shorthair. His sleek body, angular head and large flaring ears make him appear unique and exotic.

Dexter the Cat

oriental shorthairs DO have fur!

① Draw a circle and oval.

small circle head

angled oval body

② Connect head and body as shown.

add tiny circle for the chin

③ Add circle for hind leg.

angled guides

draw a light guide for the eyes, nose & mouth

overlap →

④ Add front leg and paw.

erase dotted area

⑤ Draw eyes on the top guideline.

erase dotted lines

⑥ Add nose & curved tail.

add pointy triangles for ears

overlap →

⑦ Round out the ears & add a curved mouth.

add other legs behind body

erase dotted lines

⑧ Add pupils & whiskers. Erase dotted areas.

⑨ Shade whatever color or pattern desired.

Dex is gray with green eyes

oriental shorthairs come in hundreds of colors and patterns

Create a Tattoo

Tattooing has been practiced around the world for thousands of years, reflecting a human need to decorate the body. Tattoos can have a sacred, religious, medicinal and social significance...or just be pretty designs.

The next few pages will put your imagination to the test! Pretend you are a custom tattoo artist at "Dexter's Tattoo Shop". You will be able to choose a specific client and create a colorful and imaginative piece from scratch for them based on their artistic requests. There are a variety of subjects to choose from so pick something that is interesting to you. Following the client list there is a template of a forearm outline on which the design will be created. Feel free to use this or draw a different body part outline in which the tattoo will be placed. Choose your client and take into consideration their age and interests. This will help you to design the perfect tattoo for them.

Notes:

  • Your client has offered an idea of what they want but it is up to you to make a one-of-a-kind design.

  • Use clear, crisp, even lines to create the artwork. Any shading should be steady and consistent.

  • Make sure the design is pleasant to look at – your client will have this art on their body forever!

  • Any words used in a tattoo must be spelled correctly. If you aren't sure about the spelling or meaning of a word – look it up.

  • After you've decided upon a design, determine if it will be colorful or shaded in black.

  • Remember, you are designing this artwork for someone else based upon their request. Your job is to make the client happy!

DEXTER'S TATTOO CLIENT SHEET

Choose a client below then design a tattoo based upon their request on the template provided.

1. A 45-year-old woman is getting her first tattoo. She wants something small, yet colorful, to represent her time living in Tokyo, Japan.

2. 24-year-old man asks for a tattoo that represents his career as an apple farmer.

3. 32-year-old woman comes in and asks for a tattoo that represents her job as lobster fisherwoman.

4. An artist/author/teacher requests a tattoo that represents her cat Dexter as well as her twin baby daughters born this year.

5. A young lady wants a tattoo that represents the spa she works at. Her specialty is manicures.

6. 28-year-old man wants a tattoo that represents his favorite hobby, playing chess.

7. A woman requests a tattoo that represents her favorite vacation destination, the beach.

8. A middle-aged man wants a tattoo that represents his favorite pastime, hiking through the woods.

9. A 22-year-old woman requests a tattoo to represent her boyfriend who is a guitarist in a band.

10. A man requests a tattoo in honor of his wife who is a botanist (a person who studies plants and flowers).

11. A 41-year-old wants a tattoo that represents his five cats. They are all Siamese pure bred.

12. A 65-year-old woman wants a tattoo that represents surfing in the Pacific Ocean.

13. A 26-year-old man wants a tattoo that represents his career as a builder. His specialty is framing houses.

14. A 38-year-old woman wants a tattoo to represent the grand opening of her cupcake shop.

15. A 32-year-old man wants a tattoo that represents his career as a caterer and chef.

16. An 85-year-old woman wants a tattoo that represents her greatest interest, astronomy.

17. A 41-year-old man requests a tattoo that represents his hobby as a bee keeper.

18. A grandfather requests a tattoo that commemorates his career as a computer genius.

19. A 29-year-old woman wants a tattoo that represents her favorite hobby; playing video games.

20. A young man who has several tattoos already wants a new tattoo to represent his scrap metal business named "Recycle Pros".

21. A grandmother comes in and requests a tattoo that represents the over 40 years she worked as a nurse in the Neonatal Intensive Care Unit.

ARTIST NAME :_____

DATE :_____

CUSTOMER # :_____

LOCATION OF TATTOO :_____ forearm _____

(wrist)

(elbow)

DEXTER'S
Tattoo Shop
123 HOW TO DRAW AVENUE, COOL STUFF, U.S.A.

HUMAN FACE PROFILE

KNOW:
The simple steps to create a human face

UNDERSTAND:
• The use of proportion and guidelines to create a head and generic facial features.
• Subtle differences in the shape and size of specific features that make us look unique
• Protruding objects (nose, lips, etc.) create shadows.
• The human head can be measured/created on a grid.

DO:
• Practice drawing a generic human face/head using the proposed techniques.
• Start with guide lines, place the features, shade.

NOTE:
Details on how to draw a human face and creating self portraits can be found in "How to Draw Cool Stuff: A Drawing Guide for Teachers and Students." This lesson offers a quick review of how to draw features of the face but focuses more on creating a generic face to use as a base for creating a design on top of it.

VOCABULARY:
Guidelines – A lightly marked line used as a guide when composing a drawing.

Proportion – The comparative sizes and placement of one part to another.

Human Face Profile

1. Lightly draw a circle with an overlapping, angled oval. These will be the profile guidelines.

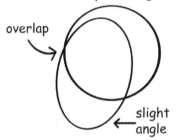

overlap

slight angle

2. Erase areas inside as shown. Add curved neck lines.

3. Lightly draw three angled lines as guides. Draw a backwards "C" for the ear.

4. Add a nose between the top & middle guide. Add the upper lip beneath it.

Erase outer guide-lines

5. Add the bottom lip & extend the chin line beyond the guideline.

Erase outer guide-lines

6. Add an arch on the top guide for the brow, a triangle beneath for the eye and a nostril.

7. Add eye detail and a line to indicate cheek. Extend earlobe.

8. Lightly sketch the hair outline and cheekbone detail.

Notice the hair is not flat/stuck to head

9. Darken the eye, brow upper lip, under nose, under neck, ear and hair areas.

SELF PORTRAIT WITH TEXT

KNOW:
Aspects of identity, Self-portrait

UNDERSTAND:
• Methods of conveying one's identity through artwork using symbols and text.
• Identity is multi-faceted and may change over time.
• Symbols have different meanings for different viewers.
• Symbols can change meaning if put in different contexts.
• Art can be for oneself and/or a method of communication.

DO:
Students will brainstorm at least 10 words/images that represent their identity, transfer the outline of their chosen head silhouette and personalize it by adding text, images, colors and quotes in a creative manner to "fill" the head.

TIPS:
• Write words and draw images close to the edge of your profile outline so it they take on the shape of that outline.
• Use different fonts/typefaces to add interest.
• Try to include an equal amount of text and images for balance and interest.

VOCABULARY:
Identity – The sense of self; the distinguishing character or personality of an individual.

Self-Portrait - A portrait of oneself, done by oneself.

Silhouette – The shape or outline of something, void of detail in the middle.

Typeface/Font - A set of letters, numbers, etc., that are all in the same style used in printing or writing.

Essential Questions:
• Who are you?
• How do you know who you are?
• What makes me – me?
• How can I share/show who I am with others?
• What symbol can I create that represents who I am now or who I desire to become?
• Who is my art for? (Who is my viewer/who is my audience?)

These steps are only an example. Use your OWN answers for "Who am I"

Text Self Portrait

1. Brainstorm at least 10 answers to the question "Who am I ?"

1. animal lover
2. part of a family
3. runner
4. reader
5. artist
6. internet surfer
7. shoppper
8. napper
9. dreamer
10. swimmer

2. Outline a face profile or have your friend trace your own profile

3. Write or draw one of your words inside of the head shape

If writing, use block, bubble or other types of letters that are not "stick" letters

FAMILY

4. Add another word or image from the list . . .

FAMILY

5. and another. Notice how the letters curve around the profile.

ZZZZZ
FAMILY

6. Keep adding images and words inside the profile

ZZZZZ
FAMILY

7. Fill entire head. Add designs or other interesting items that describe yourself for filler.

8. Color or shade

205

HUMAN HEAD

KNOW:
The simple steps to create a human face

UNDERSTAND:
• The use of proportion to create a head and generic features.
• Subtle difference in the shape and size of specific features make us look unique.
• Protruding objects (nose, lips, etc.) create shadows.
• The human head can be measured/created on a grid.

DO:
• Practice drawing a generic human face/head using the proposed techniques.
• Start with guide lines, place the features, shade.

NOTE: Details on how to draw a human face and creating self-portraits can be found in "How to Draw Cool Stuff: A Drawing Guide for Teachers and Students." This lesson offers a quick review of how to draw features of the face but focuses more on creating a generic face to use as a base for creating a design on top of it.

VOCABULARY:

Proportion – The comparative sizes and placement of one part to another.

Self-Portrait - A portrait of oneself, done by oneself.

A Basic Human Face

1. Start with an oval or "upside down" egg shape. The top part should be slightly fuller.

2. Make a lower case letter "t" in the center of the face.

3. Put your finger in the center of the "t" and your other finger on the chin. Find the center and draw a line there. This will be the bottom of the nose.

4. Put your finger in the center of the line you just made and your other finger on the chin. Find the middle, make one last line. This will be the mouth.

5. On the top line, draw two almond/football shapes for the eyes. TIP: The distance between your eyes is about the width of one eye.

6. Add the iris, pupil, eyelids, etc. On the second line, draw the bottom of the nose. TIP: The width of the bottom of the nose is about the same as the width between the eyes.

A Basic Human Face
. . . continued

⑦.

Add "spokes" in the iris and lines for the brows and sides of the nose. TIP #1: The sides of your nose are connected to your brows! TIP #2: The fattest part of the nose is the base, the thinnest part is between the brows. (think triangle shaped)

⑧.

Start the lips. The mouth is usually as wide as the distance between the pupils.
TIP: Don't forget to add the "Cupid's Bow": the little divit at the top of the upper lip.

⑨.

Add the neck lines.
TIP: The neck is about as wide as the edges of the mouth lines.
Add the bottom lip.
TIP: The bottom is usually fuller than the upper on MOST people.

⑩

Add the hairline (looks like a swim cap). Add the ears.
TIP: The top of the ear lines up with the eye line, the bottom of the ear lines up with the bottom of the nose.

⑪

Erase the guidelines.

⑫

Add a hair style.

CVH

208

DESIGNING SUGAR SKULLS

KNOW:
Dia de los Muertos, Sugar Skull, Symmetry

UNDERSTAND:
• The use of proportion and guidelines to create a head and generic features.
• The meaning and uses of sugar skulls related to Mexican culture.
• Popular designs used when creating sugar skulls.

DO:
• Practice drawing a generic human face/head using the proposed techniques.
• Explore the tradition of using and decorating sugar skulls, then, create an original sugar skull composition based on popular designs.

TIPS: The symbolism of a sugar skull is rooted in the decoration around the eyes. Flowers are meant to symbolize life, while cob webs symbolize death. Burning candles set inside the eyes are a sign of remembrance. These items can also be used in combination to personalize the main focus of the skull as well. If you're having trouble coming up with ideas on how to adorn your sugar skull, just choose designs or images that you like or check out the ideas on page 203.

NOTES: These tutorials show a few popular ideas for creating sugar skull compositions on a female face and a male face followed by an idea page which offers some other popular sugar skull designs. A basic human face and basic skull tutorial are also included. Following the tutorials are templates that can be copied in order to draw designs directly onto in the case that the artist does not want to draw the human face or skull as a base.

VOCABULARY:
Dia de los Muertos – A traditional holiday on November 1st and 2nd where Mexican families celebrate the lives of their dearly departed friends and relatives.

Sugar Skull – Sugar skulls are art pieces often made in Mexico created using molded sugar, feathers, beads, foil and icing to decorate gravestones in celebration of The Day of the Dead (Dia de los Muertos). Sugar skulls are made from very few ingredients - sugar, meringue powder, and water. The mixture is pressed into a mold and allowed to dry, creating a plain white three-dimensional skull. The artistic part of sugar skull creation is how it's decorated once the molded skull is formed.

Symmetry – The parts of an image or object organized so that one side duplicates or mirrors the other.

Sugar skulls are art pieces created using molded sugar, feathers, beads, and icing to decorate gravestones on The Day of the Dead.

Sugar Skull Girl

1. Start with a basic face outline. Draw a circular shape around the eye area to indicate eye sockets of a skull. Embellish with a design around it.

2. Outline the nose so it resembles the shape of a skull nose area. This is basically an inverted triangle near the bridge of the nose.

3. Next, add a design on the chin area. This is often shown as a flower shape.

4. Indicate cheekbones using swirls, spiderwebs or dark colors blended down toward the jawline.

5. Draw "stitches" across the mouth area up towards the cheeks. Add a swirl or spiderweb design on the forehead.

6. Color in the design using contrasting shades so the features really stand out. Add lots of "extras".

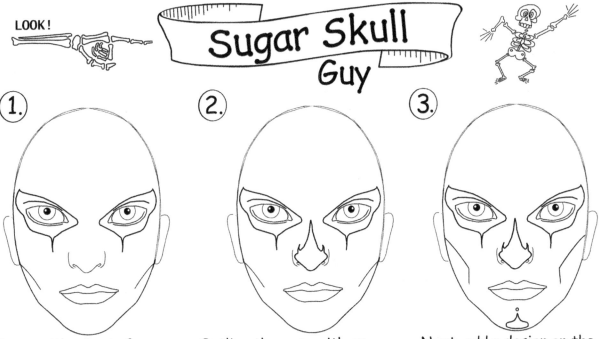

Sugar Skull Guy

①.

Start with a basic face. Draw an interesting shape around the eye area to highlight it. This will later be shaded in with a dark color.

②.

Outline the nose with an upside-down triangular shape. This can be embellished to make it look more interesting.

③.

Next, add a design on the chin area. On males, this is often shown as a simple geometric shape, spiderweb or swirl.

④.

Draw "stitches" across the mouth area. These lines should extend beyond the mouth and stretch towards the cheek area.

⑤.

Add simple shapes, swirls or spiderwebs to the forehead. Embellish as desired.

⑥.

Color in the design using contrasting shades so the features really stand out. Add lots of "extras".

Sugar Skull Ideas

Dia De Los Muertos is a ritual about paying respects to loved ones who have passed away. In Mexico, November 1st is dedicated as Dia De Los Inocentes, a day to honor and respect children and infants. November 2nd is Dia De Los Muertos, the day to honor deceased adults.

Below are some popular ideas that have been used to create certain features on sugar skulls. Sugar skulls are molds made from sugar in the shape of a skull used to represent a departed soul. Keep in mind, there are millions of designs that can be created - this is just a small sampling!

Some options for a nose decoration . . .

Eyes . . .

Forehead designs . . .

Mouth options . . .

Chin options . . .

Embellish other areas with roses, swirls, dots and flowers . . .

THE HUMAN SKULL

KNOW:
• Balance, Proportion and Symmetry

UNDERSTAND:
• Simple drawing steps used to create a realistic human skull.
• Major bones of the head.
• Features of the human head can be measured/created on a grid.

DO:
• Practice drawing a generic human face/head using the proposed techniques.
• Start with guide lines, place the features, shade.

VOCABULARY:
Balance – The way an artwork is arranged to create a feeling of stability; a pleasing or harmonious arrangement or proportion of parts or areas in a design or composition.

Cranium – Portion of the skull that encloses the braincase.

Human Skull - Supports the structures of the face and forms a cavity for the brain.

Mandible – The lower jawbone.

Proportion – The comparative sizes and placement of one part to another.

Symmetry - Parts of an image or object organized so that one side duplicates or mirrors the other; the same on both sides.

Draw a Human Skull

1. Start with a circle.

2. Add a rectangle.

erase dotted area

3. Add jawline.

angle lines at points

4. Round edges.

add curve

round and erase sharp edges

5. Add eyes, nose and mouth.

add eyes

"house" shaped nose

smile

6. Define the mouth area.

erase dotted areas

add "arrow" points

add two slightly curved "teeth" lines

7. Add details as shown.

curve tops of teeth

brow ridges

inner nose detail

add teeth

8. Smooth out the hard lines.

Smooth out the hard edges and round off any pointed lines

DRAW SOMETHING WICKED

KNOW:
• You can create a complex, original character by using simple, geometric shapes
• Adding details and embellishments to a generic drawing can make a unique artwork

UNDERSTAND:
• To make a work original, that work must have elements that are not copied or traced.
• Expressive qualities in your drawing add a feeling, mood or idea to your character.
• A detailed backstory describing the character you create adds interest.

DO:
Practice creating an original character using the provided samples as inspiration. Draw lightly so guidelines can be erased if needed. Add or change certain elements as necessary to make it unique. Combine several elements seen in the lesson or make up your own to create a character, name and story NOT seen on the handout. Use your imagination and add a lot of "extras".

TIPS:
• Choose a name for your character. This will help to personalize him or her.
• Think about the kind of impact you want your creature to have. Decide what its goals are and why it looks the way it does.
• Accessories can be a huge part of your character. Take time to plan the little "extras" your character is wearing or uses.
• Develop the creature's history and background: where it came from, how it was created and why it acts the way it does.
• To get inspiration, take a peek at the sample characters and body parts in this lesson, but put your own spin on them to make it original!

VOCABULARY:
Expressive Qualities - The feelings, moods and ideas communicated to the viewer through a work of art.

Original – Any work considered to be an authentic example of the works of an artist, rather than a reproduction, imitation or a copy.

This is a list of ideas for your creature . . . use parts that you like and make up the rest!

Draw Something Wicked
part I

1. Choose a head shape. There are thousands to create - these are just a few . . .

pointy

oval

furry

exposed brain

bumpy

2. Next, create an expressive set of eyes (or just one eye - you pick!)

rolled back

giant pupil

skinny pupil

no pupil

reptile-like

two eyes in one

round reptile

tube

drippy

angry

surprised

claw lashes

3. Choose a scary mouth. Extra points for lots of teeth and dripping saliva!

pointy smiles

foamy vomit

cracked

wide open

toothy worm

underbite fangs

vampire fangs

clenching teeth

happy pointers

Draw Something Wicked
part II

4. Pick a nose ;)

nose ring

warty

beak-like

three nostrils

skull nose

turned-up

a bit piggy

more piggy

skeletal

canine

5. Create a body. Again, there are millions of shapes and sizes to choose from - these are just a few!

short

round

top heavy

bottom heavy

tall triangular

big head

pear shaped

stick person

fuzzy fella

Sin-derella

A former beauty queen, SinDerella lurks in the cemetery after midnight to dig up the buried and steal their jewelry.

worms in hair

dirt on face

dripping with jewels

spider webs

shovel for digging

purse full of jewels and a ringed hand

missing shoe

Hector the Hip-Hop Zombie

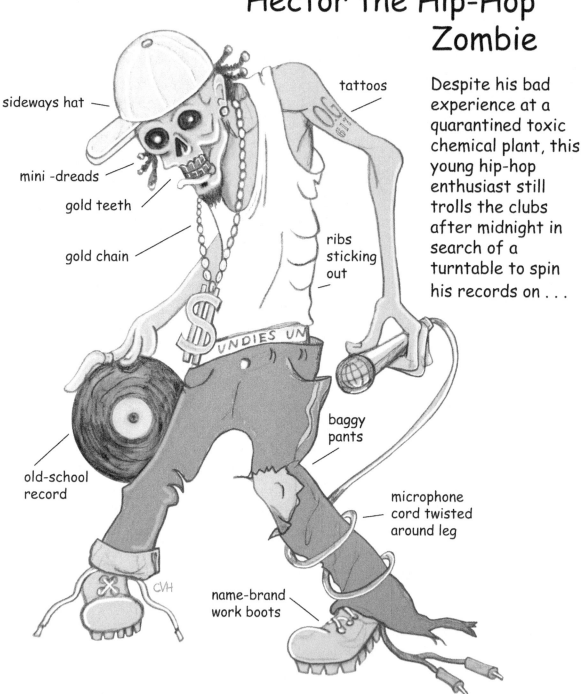

sideways hat

mini -dreads

gold teeth

gold chain

tattoos

ribs sticking out

Despite his bad experience at a quarantined toxic chemical plant, this young hip-hop enthusiast still trolls the clubs after midnight in search of a turntable to spin his records on . . .

old-school record

baggy pants

microphone cord twisted around leg

name-brand work boots

Chef S'morgue

Chef S'morgue wants to cater your party! Eyeball skewers, foamed lizard toe, bat bowel bile, and candied fingers are on the menu. Hope you're hungry . . .

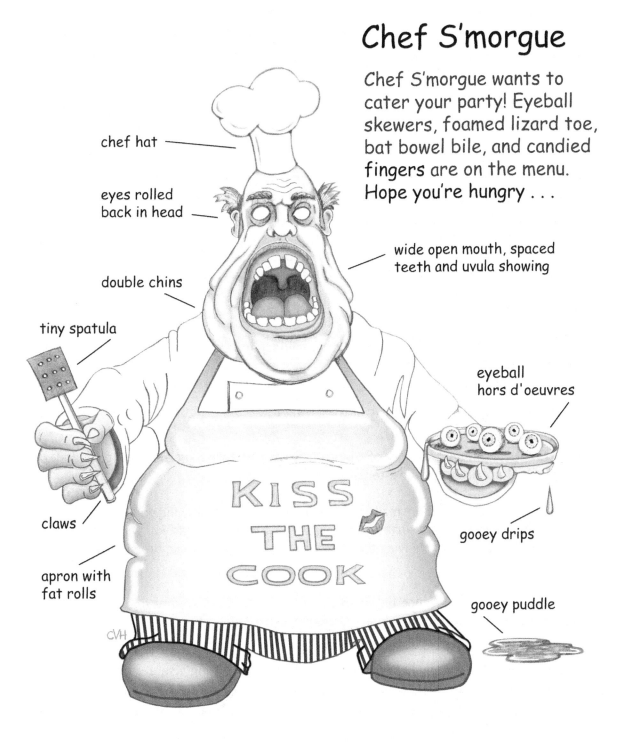

chef hat

eyes rolled back in head

double chins

tiny spatula

claws

apron with fat rolls

wide open mouth, spaced teeth and uvula showing

eyeball hors d'oeuvres

gooey drips

gooey puddle

KISS THE COOK

KITTY CAT FACE
on black paper

KNOW:
• Texture
• Drawing using white media on a dark surface
• Using contrast in drawings is a great way to create a dynamic image. One way of creating good contrast is by using white material or media on dark or black surfaces
• Black paper offers a number of challenges but also provides some interesting alternative approaches

UNDERSTAND:
• Recognize the importance of tints (lighter values) and their inherent relationships with shades (darker values).
• With practice, our understanding of value and how it is used to create drawings will improve.
• Creating intense contrast.

DO: Create an original artwork of a large kitty cat face following the steps provided. Use shading and texture to create interest.

TIP: (If using black paper) Normally, when you are creating a drawing you would draw with dark material onto a white surface. This process is the opposite as you will be adding light values to the surface and leaving the dark values alone, almost like drawing in reverse.

VOCABULARY:
Contrast – A large difference between two things; for example, hot and cold. This term refers to a way of juxtaposing elements of art to stress the differences between them.

Layer – Something placed over another surface.

Overlap - When one thing lies over, partly covering something else. Depicting this is one of the most important means of conveying an illusion of depth.

Invert – To reverse the order or condition of something such as when making what is black white, and what is white black.

Texture - The way something looks like it might feel like in an artwork. Simulated textures are suggested by an artist with different brushstrokes, pencil lines, etc.

Try using white pastel on black paper!

Kitty Cat Face

A cat has 230 bones in its body. A human has 206.

1.

Start with two "football" oval shapes - Place the ovals about 1/3 of the way down from the top of your paper.

2. Add two skinny ovals inside the "footballs".

Add a capital letter "T" for the nose

3.

Curve in the sides of the "T" Add a "W" touching the bottom of the "T" shape.

4.

Add a 1/2 circle at chin area Add nostrils.

5. Cats have 130,000 hairs per square inch. We will draw just a few.

Shade above nose →
Close the nose →
Curve around eye area

SHADE LIGHTLY!

6.

Lightly shade nose cheeks & chin.

tiny fur lines

7. Color the eyes.

a. black pupil with yellow outside

b. blend brown at top & sides

c. blend green around pupil

d. Add white highlights

8.

Add curved whiskers coming from cheek area (some short, some long)

9.

CAf

RUBE GOLDBERG INSPIPRED MACHINE

KNOW:
• Process of Invention
• Rube Goldberg
• "Cause and Effect"
• Motions, Forces and Transfer of Energy

UNDERSTAND:
• Students will better understand how machine parts can work together to create a simple task.
• Understand Newton's Laws of Motion.
• Abilities of technical design.
• Backwards planning to accomplish a goal.
• How to design, problem solve, and illustrate a simple machine.

DO:
• Observe, read and interpret examples of Rube Goldberg Machines.
• Students will decide what simple everyday task their machine will complete, then design a device using at least 10 different items that accomplishes that task using maximum effort to achieve minimal results.
• Students will create an explanation of what task their device accomplishes or write a creative story that incorporates their new device.

TIP: The process of invention requires beginning with the end goal, or the last thing that needs to happen. Decide what the goal should be, then begin working backward, creating as many steps as possible to accomplish the final task.

When creating the machine, ask questions such as: "Can this object launch or move that object?" or "Will this object roll?" This will help to decide what items to use to accomplish the task. Write down a list of any possible objects to use that will help.

VOCABULARY:
Action – When something done or performed; the accomplishment of a thing, usually over a period of time in stages.

Device – A thing made for a particular purpose.

Invent – To create with the imagination or produce a product of one's own ingenuity, experimentation, or contrivance; to create or produce (something useful) for the first time.

Energy – Exertion of power.

Rube Goldberg - Pulitzer Prize-winning cartoonist who is best known for his "invention" cartoons which use a series of steps and objects to accomplish everyday simple tasks in the most complicated way. Goldberg's drawings point out that people are often overwhelmed by overcomplicating their lives.

"Machine" Parts

1. Draw a conveyor belt to move items from one area to another.

2. A roll of tape can be used to roll into an item when pushed or it can stick to things.

3. A ball can roll down a chute and knock something over.

4. A spray can can be activated to create wind or make something sticky.

5. A candle can be lit to burn through piece of string.

6. A bird can fly away with something.

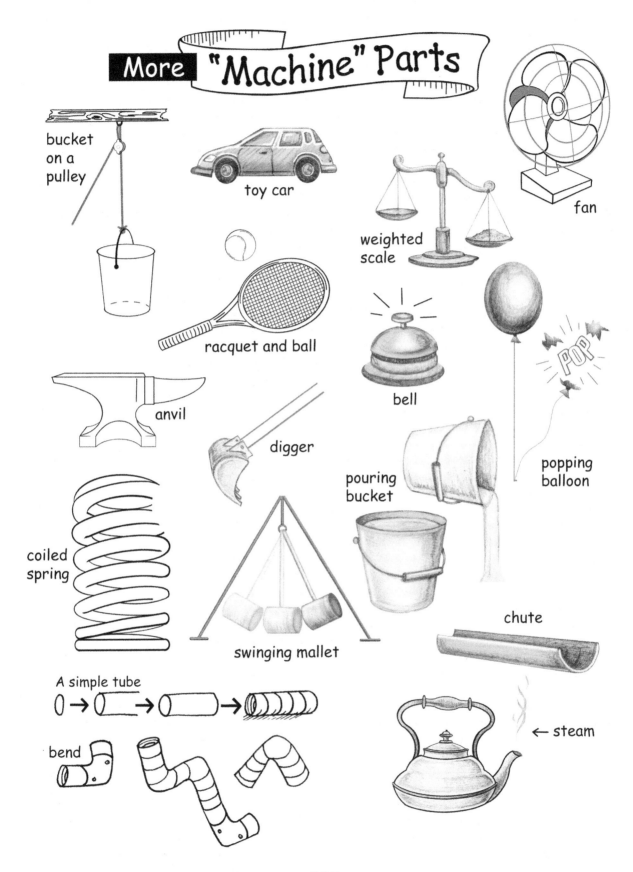

More "Machine" Parts

bucket on a pulley

toy car

weighted scale

fan

racquet and ball

bell

popping balloon

anvil

digger

pouring bucket

coiled spring

swinging mallet

chute

A simple tube

bend

← steam

Dexter's Dinner Machine

1. Feed bird
2. Scale tips & pushes lever
3. Fan turns on
4. Fan blows nail
5. Balloon pops . . .
6. . . . releasing the hammer
7. Pushing the car
8. Match strikes
9. Candle lights & burns through string
10. Bucket releases & pours water into tank
11. Boat rises
12. Ball rolls down chute
13. Ball tips cat food box
14. Food pours into bowl
15. Dexter stops meowing for five minutes.

EPILOGUE

We use creativity every day in every aspect of our lives. From creative problem solving to the simple appreciation of beauty, the act of creating can provide a platform to explore experiences within yourself and help communicate information to others. One important way to do this is through art and drawing. Whether the goal is to become a skilled artist, create a likeness, express a feeling or simply to create interesting things; drawing is a great way of improving concentration, expressing individuality and providing pleasure for yourself.

The ability to draw is a skill that is learned, not a gift we are born with. Everyone has the ability to become a skilled artist through practice and patience. The more practice, the better the outcome. Anyone has the ability to draw. The growth and improvement that is a result of creating never stops as long as there is a desire to create. The lessons in "How to Draw Cool Stuff" offer guidelines to follow for the creation of specific objects. This does not necessarily mean these ideas should be copied exactly as they are printed without deviation from the original. Sometimes it is necessary to copy when first learning how to draw a specific object, even tracing can be an acceptable practice as one is learning how to draw. However, it is important not to be too concerned with trying to make your drawing look just like the one in the book. Your unique (and sometimes imperfect) approach is what will make an artwork engaging and beautiful. It can be significant to see what will happen when creating a work of art rather than to make something specific happen. An idea that you start with can turn into something completely different. If this begins to happen, let it. Create whatever your art desires without the pressure of doing things like everyone else.

Once an artist becomes engaged in the process of creating, beautiful and unique things can happen. Oftentimes, the process of creating is even more valuable than the outcome. The act of drawing can offer an escape from reality, a way to pass the time, a way to relax and become something enjoyable to do.

It is important to explore and experiment as you draw. One obstacle that is difficult to overcome as you draw is the idea of what other people think of your work or comparing your work to another person's art. Try not to do this. What you have to offer is what makes an artwork interesting. There may be times that you feel stuck in your progress or blocked from proceeding any further. This happens to everyone. If you feel like you are getting stuck, take a break and have patience with yourself. The unique path one person takes while creating can be very different from someone else's. That is the beauty of art. We all have different ideas, methods and approaches to drawing and that is what makes art so wonderful. Forget about the idea of needing so-called talent or gaining accolades and awards for your work. Just draw. When participating in the process of creating without rigid expectations or preconceptions, the power of drawing comes alive.

Creativity is a part of our everyday lives. Art fosters the need for creative problem solving, innovation, reasoning creatively and envisioning multiple solutions to dilemmas. These skills are beneficial to employers and colleges but are also necessary in life. Most importantly, having a creative outlet makes us happy. Make time in your week to spend a bit of time drawing your own "cool stuff" and don't worry about the final product. Enjoy the journey!

Made in the USA
Middletown, DE
13 May 2021